WHERE'S MY HUSBAND?

Ending the cycles of Marriage and Divorce

Bringing Hope, Healing, and a Fresh Beginning

TERRI LYNNE CORBETT

Where's My Husband?

By Terri Lynne Corbett
Copyright © 2017, 2018, 2023

ISBN: 154537211X
ISBN: 9781545372111

Unless otherwise noted, Bible quotations are taken from The King James Version (KJV); Copyright © 1982, Thomas Nelson, Inc.; The Amplified Bible (AMP); Copyright © 1987, The Zondervan Corporation and the Lockman Foundation.

Published in the United States of America
By Where's My Husband Publishing
Beulah, Michigan 2018

First Edition
Printed in the United States of America

WHAT READERS ARE SAYING ABOUT

TERRI CORBETT: WHERE'S MY HUSBAND?

"You never know what you've lost until you realize you haven't found it. Terri takes us through searching for satisfaction through relationships and learns that Christ is the first answer. While not everyone experiences multiple marriages to find Christ, we all relate to needing to find him, no matter when. Through Terri's intricate relational experiences, she demonstrates how we all continue to look for someone or some sin until we realize it's a God sized hole".

-Kim Clark - MA LPCS NBCC Owner Private Practices
Certified Life Coach, Telehealth Counselor
Grace Counseling Professionals, Joy Counseling

"Wow! Your heart for this message is so obvious, passionate, and precious. This message is unique and will touch the hearts of those who specifically need it. We are very familiar with THAT territory, right? Terri has a personal passion for helping those who have experienced the heartbreak of a broken marriage. This book shares her personal healing journey and offers the reader firsthand hope for healing and restoration. God has a plan, and a message of healing and hope for every particular heartbreak. Thank you for sharing this one. Stay the course friend, He will guide your way!"

-Pat Layton – Founder, President, Author, Speaker, and Coach
Life Impact Network 501(c)3
Surrendering the Secret

"The story is raw and honest with redemptive value as the author shares her personal journey. Through brokenness and pain, she allows a relationship with God to bring restoration to the most vulnerable places of her heart. It's hard to put down once you start reading. The life-giving words are inspiring and challenge women to put God first and foremost so they can be healthy and whole in whatever stage of life they're in."

-Nadine Helmuth Patton
Author of Angels on Assignment:
Adventures on the Farm (Vol. 1)

"Terri's book, Where's My Husband? is a real page turner of suspense and anticipation. I was on the edge of my seat through her trials and sighing with relief when her Wonderful Wayne came back into her life for good. What a love story. I was awed by the Lord's redemptive love for her and how He kept Terri through five husbands. I was challenged by her candid honesty and found myself examining my own heart for evidence of her kind of courage. I loved her vulnerability and faith in action, knowing that if Jesus is always there for her, He's always there for me too. Terri is proof that no matter what your past has been, God has a way for you through the wilderness of broken dreams and broken promises."

-Carol Osgrove
Author of Texting to Heaven
Speaker Stonecroft Ministries

Table of Contents

Dedication

First and foremost, to my wonderful Husband Wayne, who peeled back the onion one layer at a time, instilling in me from the very beginning the DON'T QUIT attitude. Thanks for your patient endurance with me while writing the book, and especially as I heal and mature in the Lord. You are my rock and I love you dearly.

To my beloved sons. Thank you for your resilience and sense of humor, but above all else your love and forgiveness. I am so proud of you both.

To Dr. Bruce Hitchcock for an enlightening Foreword about Redemption, Justification, and Transformation through Jesus Christ. I am truly blessed for your writing guidance and direction.

To my kind friend Si Osgrove for the many hours spent editing this book, and your writing expertise. You are a treasure.

To my author friends, Carol Osgrove and Nadine Patton Helmuth. Thank you for sharing your experiences, your heartfelt words of encouragement, and your passion for bringing God's love to others. I'm honored to know you both.

To my dearest friends and family, who after learning of my past didn't judge me, but loved me instead. Thank you for your love and prayers.

To the brave women and men who with courage choose hope and to Declare Their SOUL TO BELIEVE and Their ENEMY TO LEAVE! To all the family and friends struggling to understand those who have been married and divorced multiple times.

Foreword
By Dr. Bruce Hitchcock

As I read through the pages of Terri Corbett's' book transcript "Where's My Husband?" two thoughts ran through my mind. The first is the words to the country western song "Lookin' for Love."

> Well, I've spent a lifetime lookin' for you;
>
> singles bars and good time lovers were never true.
>
> Playin' a fool's game hopin' to win;
>
> and tellin' those sweet lies and losin' again.
>
> I was lookin' for love in all the wrong places,
>
> Lookin' for love in too many faces,
>
> searchin' their eyes and lookin' for traces
>
> of what I'm dreamin' of.[1]

This 1980's song, sung by country singer Johnny Lee was a huge crossover hit. Probably because it was true in so many people's lives. Many people spend a lifetime looking for love in all the wrong places.

The second thought that ran through my mind was the biblical

---

1   Johnny   Lee,   play.google.com/music/preview/Tbf3xnqlss4dqcfe   pbbuuqh dkmy?lyrics=1&utm_source=google&utm_medium=search&utm_campaign=lyrics& pcampaignid=kp-lyrics&u=0#

account of Jesus and the Samarian woman at the well.

On His way from Judea to Galilee, Jesus passed through Samaria. This was an unusual route since the Jews and the Samaritans hated each other (John 4:1-4). As Jesus reached Samaria, He stopped at Jacob's well (John 4:5-6).

At the well, Jesus met a woman who was there to draw water. Jesus addressed the women by saying, *"Give me to drink."* Then the woman, understanding the hatred between her people and the Jews, asked Jesus, *"How is it that thou, being a Jew, askest drink of me, which am a woman of Samaria?"* (John 4:7-9).

Jesus responded that If she knew who was speaking, she would have asked for *"living water."* The woman then asked Jesus, where He was going to get this *"living water."* He had nothing with Him to draw water and the well is deep. Then she continued by asking Jesus if He was greater than their father Jacob who had given them the well (John 4:10-12).

With great patience and compassion, Jesus answered and said that those who drink the well water will thirst again, but those who drink the water Jesus provides will never thirst again since His water is a spring within them that provides eternal life. Immediately, she asks for this water so that she will not have to make the long trip every day. She did not understand the spiritual significance of Christ's offer (John 4:13-15).

Jesus told her to go and get her husband. This request opens the spiritual door to salvation. The woman at the well responded that she had no husband. Jesus explained that she is telling the truth. Then He points out that she has had five husbands and the one she is currently living with is not her husband.

At this point the woman is under the conviction from the Holy Spirit and tries to change the subject. She knows that she is living a life of sin. Jesus explains that the time is coming when they will neither be required to worship in the mountain or in Jerusalem. Instead they will all worship the Father in Spirit and in Truth (John 4:16-24).

Now we reach the climax of the story. The woman says that she knows that when Messiah comes He will speak all truth from God. Jesus responds, *"I am the Messiah."* (John 4:25-26).

This is an incredible story of the truth of salvation. Redemption, justification, and transformation come only through the blood of Jesus. Here in this great story we see all three. First, we see the offer of redemption. The woman at the well was living in sin and had been for many years. She needed a redeemer, a spiritual redeemer. Jesus was that redeemer. He had not yet shed the blood of redemption from the beatings in the court to the cross of sacrifice. However, He had committed to that act before the foundation of the world. Jesus was therefore qualified to offer redemption to this woman.

Secondly, Jesus was offering her justification. The blood of Jesus offers justification to all who would believe. Salvation comes by grace through faith alone (Ephesians 2:8-9). Justification is the action within salvation by which we are reconciled to God. I once heard J. Vernon McGee on his radio broadcast say, "Justification means just if I'd never sinned." We, as imperfect humans, can forgive but never forget when someone has wronged us. However, God forgives and forgets. Our past sins, now under the blood through justification will never be held against us. God has forgiven and forgotten the sins of believers (Psalm 103:12).

Finally, Jesus offered this lost but looking woman spiritual transformation. When we accept Jesus as Lord of our lives (Romans 10:9-10), we are born again (John 3:7) and we become a new creation (2 Corinthians 5:17). Just as the worm enters the cocoon and becomes a Monarch butterfly, we are completely transformed into a new creature (Galatians 6:15). We are now free from the bondage of sin (Galatians 5:1). Free to choose to be good or bad (Galatians 5:13).

Jesus knew this woman and her sins, just as He knows all our sins. Choosing the issue of her five marriages was not an accident. Jesus knew it was her Achilles heel. He knew that she was searching for a love relationship that cannot exist outside of God.

We all make bad decisions since we are by nature sinful and unrighteous (Psalm 14:3-6, Romans 3:10-18). We all deserve eternal separation and punishment from God (Romans 3:23).

The Woman at the Well was shunned by society. The pain and suffering of her life of bad decisions ran deep. She was in the throngs of sin by living in an adulterous relationship. She knew that what she was doing was wrong. That is why she changed the subject when she was confronted with her immoral social situation.

This woman, despite her social standing, knew the message of the Old Testament. She knew that God would send a Messiah (Savior, Deliverer) who would know all truth.

Despite her life and her sin, Jesus offered her eternal life through the message of the gospel, *"the water of the Word"* that cleanses us from all sin no matter how egregious. While she was still in her sin Jesus offered her complete vindication (Romans 5:8). No sin is so great that God cannot forgive us. No life is so deep in sin that we cannot be transformed.

The woman at the well was undoubtedly scorned and rejected for her lifestyle choices. Society today is no different. People may not accept a woman who has been married five times. However, God will, and He did.

Just as the woman at the well was *"looking for love in all the wrong places,"* so was Terri Lynne Corbett. Her early childhood experience of rejection, abuse, family repudiation and scorn led to a lifelong search for love. Because of the warped and distorted view of family and love that she experienced as the youngest child in a dysfunctional family, she made many poor choices as she matured.

The imperfect choices that Terri made led to pain and eventually to anger. Relying on herself to make her life better only caused deeper anguish and shame. She was living the nightmare of codependency with people who had perverted sense of love and relationship.

It was only when she was drawn to God in her deepest moments of depression that she finally found true love. The love that is greater, deeper, and more meaningful than any worldly love. Terri realized that before you can find a meaningful, lasting love relationship with another person, you must first fall in love with God. God's love is not sensual or emotional love, but unconditional, eternal love (Psalm 36:5-7, Psalm 52:8, Jeremiah 31:3, Romans 8:35, Ephesians 3:17-19).

Once Terri had found this love, she understood true love. When she began focusing on God as the center of her life and understood that measure of a relationship, she was ready to love again. God in his goodness brought Terri's fifth husband, also a believer, back into her life. The consequences of their new relationship with Jesus allowed them to establish a God centered, true love relationship with each other.

Terri is not alone. Many people have suffered and continue to endure a life lived like the woman at the well. According to Dr. Mark Banschick, M.D. in his article "The High Failure Rate of Second and

Third Marriages" more than half of all marriages end in divorce. However, the pain does not stop there. In an article in Psychology Today, his research shows that "67% of second, and 73% of third marriages end in divorce."2 This issue does not apply to hundreds or even thousands of people here in America, but multiple millions of those who are suffering due to multiple marriages.

This is an important book. When we consider the state of multiple divorces in America among both non-religious and religious the outward discrimination toward people involved in multiple marriages, this book has a large potential audience. The readers will not only find an "edge of your seat" autobiography, but also hear a clear statement of the gospel message and how to live a fulfilling life well-pleasing to God. This blend of explanation, confession, repentance, justification, and ultimately a sense of spiritual reality found only in the love of God will be easily identifiable to everyone who reads it.

Thank you, Terri, for giving us such an insightful, honest look at the reality of multiple marriages and explaining how only God can bring comfort and sanity out of human crisis and chaos.

---

2 Dr. Mark Banschick, M.D., The High Failure Rate of Second and Third Marriages, Psychology Today © 1991-2017 Sussex Publishers, LLC | HealthProfs.com © 2002-2017 Sussex Directories, Inc., psychologytoday.com/blog/the-intelligent-divorce/201202/the-high-failure-rate-second-and-third-marriages 3 Mark Banschick, M.D. The Intelligent Divorce, February 6, 2012, © 2017, Psychology Today psychologytoday.com

Introduction

Several years ago, I had a dream that inspired me, even gave me permission to write this book to women who have been married and divorced multiple times. Namely Christian women who have struggled with shame, identity, and searched for true love. I was conflicted with guilt and shame for years before I decided to take a good, long, honest look at myself. My hope is that you can read this book, avoid these same mistakes, and help others to not make them. After writing this book God showed me that plenty of men have travelled this road as well, and as a dear pastor once said to me, "chew up the meat and spit out the bones", so guys, use what applies and keep the rest for a friend. The Lord himself gives us this promise from His Word:

> *And I will restore to you the years that the locust hath eaten, the cankerworm, and the caterpillar, and the palmerworm, my great army which I sent among you. And ye shall eat in plenty, and be satisfied, and praise the name of the LORD your God, that hath dealt wondrously with you: and my people shall never be ashamed. And ye shall know that I am in the midst of Israel, and that I am the LORD your God, and none else: and my people shall never be ashamed (Joel 2:25-27 KJV)*

As you move through the pages of this journey with me, I'll frequently stop in the middle of a story or a thought and insert scriptures that the Lord gave me to encourage and strengthen you. These scriptures all pertain to the events and circumstances that I was going through at the time.

This book identifies certain events and words spoken throughout my lifetime that affected how I viewed myself and my relationships. My prayer is that it will help you identify some of the lies we believe that hold us back from making better decisions and ultimately, stepping into the beautiful plan that God has for our lives.

Maybe you have never been married. Maybe you know someone who has gone through the awful pains of multiple marriages and want to better recognize and understand certain behaviors of a loved one. Maybe you are a parent, loved one or even a friend who would like to help someone else avoid these pitfalls by being a support to them.

Whatever the reason you chose to read this book, I am certain that it will help to expose some of the lies of our enemy who does not want us to succeed in our calling from Christ. He will stop at nothing and we must be aware of his tactics.

I am not a doctor or a psychologist, just a woman like the woman at the well, who wanted so much to know love, but kept substituting man after man for God's true and unconditional love. I needed to Declare My SOUL TO BELIEVE and My ENEMY TO LEAVE! Once and for all, and once I did, that is where my true healing and redemption began.

If you are like me and you have experienced first-hand the cycles of shame, rejection and guilt from multiple marriages, there is hope. As you move through your own healing journey long after you have read this book, my prayer is that you will be better equipped to stop the words of your enemy and his lies and replace them with the Word of God. To avoid all the distractions and lies handcrafted just for you to destroy God's plan for your life.

If we truly do desire healing and to make better choices, we must be willing and acutely aware of being exposed to the one who knows and loves us better than anyone. Then and only then, can we begin to see where we go wrong. Honesty is always the best policy and it will free you to move forward in your healing.

> *If any of you lacks wisdom [to guide him through a decision or circumstance], he is to ask of [our benevolent] God, who gives to everyone generously and without rebuke or blame, and it will be given to him. (James 1:5 AMP)*

May God truly bless you and keep you as you move through this healing journey.

> *For I know the thoughts that I think toward you, saith the Lord, thoughts of peace, and not of evil, to give you an expected end (hope in your latter end),*

Then shall ye call upon me, and ye shall go and pray unto me, and I will hearken unto you, And ye shall seek me, and find me, when ye shall search for me WITH ALL YOUR HEART, And I will be found of you, saith the Lord: and I will turn away your captivity, and I will gather you from all the nations, and from all the places whither I have driven you, saith the Lord; and I will bring you again into the place whence I caused you to be carried away captive. (Jeremiah 29:11 KJV)

1

A Young Girl's Dream, Acceptance and Identity

I have the fondest memories of growing up in Sunny Southern California as the youngest of three sisters and one stepbrother. I was the baby and was treated like one too. It was glorious! We went on vacations that included camping and boating. We shared birthday parties, did chores, walked to school, ran track, watched TV, made up scary stories like "The Man with the Golden Arm", had crazy Halloween parties, sold World's Finest Chocolate Bars and P-Nuttles in a can, did the hide in the trunk routine to get into the drive-in theater for free, did our makeup, got tickled until we almost had an accident, fought, cried, and braided our hair. We told stories, made-up stories, played with our Barbie's, rode bikes, baked, cooked and cleaned together. We had a great time growing up, and I'm warmly certain my siblings would agree.

I guess you could say I was a bit of a 'Tom Boy' growing up. I often enjoyed adventure of a more 'spirited' nature than my three sisters and preferred boy's toys like race car tracks and Lincoln logs. I grew up with nicknames that had a tragic ring to them like, 'Terri the Terrible', 'Ornery', and 'Rotten Kid'. Family and friends used them often towards me and thought it was cute. I certainly did not! I loved climbing trees and roofs and walking the railroad tracks with my best friend very early in the morning. I also loved to build forts in the outside fields and to take long walks imagining being someone else, somewhere else.

I started smoking cigarettes at age thirteen because I thought it was cool and liked the attention of other kids who also smoked. Though thankfully I quit smoking at age thirty-one, unfortunately it caused all kinds of problems with bronchitis later as an adult.

Dinner time at the kitchen table with family was for me the most memorable of all. Us girls would kick each other under the table, and I would always do my best to make everyone laugh. I also had this sneaky little way of getting out of eating my vegetables by putting them in my mouth and then excusing myself to use the bathroom. This worked for a while until my dad caught on to me, and I had to find a new game plan. I tried hiding my vegetables under other foods, like bread or rolls, but eventually that was a bust too. Daddy was a real stickler for making sure we ate our veggies. I remember one time, against my will and better judgement, I complied to eat those lima beans Mom lovingly pushed for our good health, and suddenly and without warning, the 'lima bean fire hose' unleashed shock and surprise 'Sur La Table' ruining everyone's appetite. This wasn't pleasant for any of us, so Daddy gave up forcing the veggie routine; well, at least for a little while anyway.

We frequently took boating trips to Cat Harbor on the other side of

Catalina Island in Avalon, California. We snorkeled, dove for abalone, and just hung out for fun with our boating friends and family. One day is sharply etched in my memory. I was about eight or nine years old. It was cold, cloudy, and drizzly. I was already in somewhat of a sunken mood and felt uncomfortable about my surroundings. My Mom and Dad had been drinking beer having a good time when suddenly, Dad thought it was time to teach me how to swim, so......
he threw me overboard, in the deep end of the harbor! I immediately went under water, arms and legs thrashing about in panic. I didn't know how to swim. I was terrified and couldn't catch my breath as I tried to stay afloat. Shortly after, but not soon enough in my mind, Dad jumped in to rescue me, but as I recall, this was not a planned swimming lesson. I cried irrepressibly for what seemed like hours afterward. The remainder of the day I was long-faced and dejected. This may seem like a small thing to you, but as I look back, I see how it caused me to be untrusting in my adult life; in my adult relationships.

Overall, my childhood as I remember it was mostly happy times of ease and comfort. It seemed to me like soon after, my sisters began to leave home one by one after graduation. Eventually, it was just me at home with Mom and Dad. In my mind, I was still being pushed down the hallway in an upside-down stool by one sister, while the Green Monster (oldest sister in a green blanket with a hole in it for her eye) was chasing me as I screamed my head off! Then, suddenly, it was time to grow up.

One night after my three sisters moved out, it was just after supper and Mom and Dad were drinking hard liquor and fighting. I was about 12 or 13 years old. Dad had cornered Mom in the kitchen and was yelling at her while she was crying. I was angry and scared. I decided to run away from home. I walked the streets for a while then went to a friend's house, but she wasn't there. About three or four hours later after roaming the railroad tracks and visiting the corner store, I realized it was dark and cold outside and just wanted to be back in my own room. So, I went home. When I walked into the house, I expected my parents to be upset, instead they acted as if they didn't even know I had left. My heart sank. I could not believe they didn't say a word to me about it. I felt ignored and unimportant and wanted to leave again, but I had nowhere to go. Looking back, I see where my issue with rejection may have started.

Dad and I didn't have a close relationship. I can't tell you that I remember him reading to me, singing to me, or giving me life affirming words of comfort. He didn't offer advice about forming healthy relationships. There were no Daddy and Daughter dances or dates, long talks, or 'I'm so proud of you's'. On the other hand, there were plenty of parties with alcohol. When I made mistakes Dad often yelled at me and sometimes slapped me across the face. I felt ashamed and unforgiven.

All of us sisters had boyfriends, and all of us sisters made mistakes

23

from time to time, but I seemed to get in trouble the most as I craved the attention and validation of others no matter the cost. In school I was easily led into mischief by other kids, and took on their actions, speech, and behavior just to feel accepted. My dad's disappointment level was high back then and I thought I did my best, but let's face it, I gravitated to where the attention was, good or bad. This is just human nature, and the way God created us. Keep this in mind and watch how the puzzle pieces begin to form habits and mindsets on my journey. Be open to what God will show you about your own journey or someone close to you.

All in all, I have great memories of watching my dad work on cars, repair our boat, assemble pools, and add a room addition to the house. I remember the year that Daddy bought me my first car, it was a little Datsun B210 hatchback, blue and white, with a luggage rack on top. It reminded me of a dollhouse station wagon. I was thrilled when he brought it to me, and so proud to call it my own. That day I received a badly needed dose of 'daddy love'. I couldn't believe it. He took me down to the nearby industrial park where he taught me how to drive the stick shift. In two days, I was driving back and forth to work in Long Beach. This was a special time with my dad, and to this day I am so grateful for his sacrifice of time and money to help me on my way to adulthood. Remembering and cherishing these times proved to be an integral part of forgiveness and healing for me later in the story.

We didn't attend church regularly, but Mom sometimes sent us on the bus by ourselves to the local Presbyterian Church. It was fun, but I never understood why my parents didn't go with us. One-on-one discussions about morals and values were not Mom and Dad's natural parenting style, and we were not a Christian household. I strongly believe if these attributes were present in my childhood, likely there would have been no need for my reckless search for love.

We continued to have fun at family outings and get-togethers during the holidays, but alcohol was always present and a very normal way of life for us. Both Mom and Dad drank beer and hard liquor most of our growing up years. Mom liked to drink Black Velvet whiskey and started drinking early in the day after us girls moved out. She tried to hide it from us but was sometimes inebriated by mid-afternoon. Unfortunately, by age seventeen alcohol started to become a substitute for the thing I craved most - pure unconditional love.

In my early teens, desperate for love and affection, I began to look to boys for attention, and started a journey of bad relationships. A journey of drugs, alcohol and other forms of abuse. It was mid-afternoon on a school day, at the tender age of fourteen, when my dad unexpectedly came home from work to find me having sex with my boyfriend. He told me to get dressed, and after I did, he grabbed my arm and took me out to the backyard. He started yelling at me, then hit me hard with his whole hand against the left side of my head. The blow ultimately busted my eardrum. I was hysterical, shocked by my father's drastic and pre-meditated action. The crying, trembling, and ringing in my ear surged through into the night. As a result, I still suffer today with hearing loss and frequent ear infections. Writing about my life experiences was an emotional roller coaster as I relived them over, and over again. But I felt inspired to help others recognize and not minimize their own experiences that could contribute to forming difficult and unhealthy relationships.

There were times later when I needed help, such as a ride or money, and I was forced to call my parents. I was afraid to face my dad for fear of his shame-based reactions. He often told me I was no good.

I strongly believe that had my father and I been closer, I would not have gone astray finding the worst possible relationships. Please don't get me wrong. All in all, I think I had a wonderful upbringing compared to most, but I can clearly see how important it was for me to have a well-balanced relationship with my dad, with love affirmations to anchor my heart. I always wanted to please him but didn't know how, and he didn't know how to give the kind of affirming love this young girl desperately needed. Today I walk in forgiveness towards both me and my dad, and it has given me the freedom to let my heavenly Daddy love me as He does.

It wasn't until the end of my fifth marriage that I truly began to realize what was wrong with me and how to begin fixing my broken, fragmented heart. I'm still working on my relationship with the Lord moment by moment, but day by day I remind myself of my value in His eyes, the love I've been looking for all my life.

If most of us gals are honest, we grew up desiring to meet our Knight in Shining Armor, the one who would rescue us from... well, you fill in the blanks. I'm sure you could find something. Then we started the process to find him! Some gals are blessed to find him, some unfortunately never find him, and some are blessed to find him eventually after a lot of heartache and pain like me.

Let's look at some of the lies we believe and some reasons why we don't find Mr. Right the first time:

Lack of wisdom or teaching

> *Sucker for a cute face, a great body, or lots of money, or all the above.*

> *So what if he's not perfect, we can change him. Right?*

We have that part down! We can win them over to do things our way by our love, charm, intimacy, great cooking or even sometimes, being the 'Chameleon'. It's okay to compromise your own principles to win a potential husband. Right? Isn't he supposed to be our first ministry, top priority?

> *NO! WARNING! WARNING! WARNING! ALIENS APPROACHING! DANGER! NOTHING BUT LIES!*

Run, and run fast when you begin to think this way. You are headed for major disappointment, total let-down, and possibly a divorce. Run like the wind, fast into the arms of the One Who Will Always Love You. Jesus Christ. He's the best listener, loves to cook with you, listen to you, hear you sing, and take road trips and long walks on the beach. I know, I know. Sounds like a Match.com profile. But it's true! He is always there and desires an intimate relationship with you. Once this relationship is established and strong, and you've found your place IN HIM, then, and only then, will you be better equipped, with eyes wide open to use sound judgment in developing stronger and healthier relationships.

The messages that have been played to us all our lives have had powerful influence in forming our thoughts about life. For example, talk about ideals, such as "Be all that you can be", media hype, movies, and family members are other sources of messages that influence us. Even the deep natural longing as a woman to fulfill that desperate desire to nurture, mother, fix, and make all the bad go away may cause us to cloud our thinking and find all the right reasons, in our own minds, to make a bad decision.

Have you ever had any of the following thoughts?

> *"I know he has a temper, but he can't help it*
> *because he had a bad upbringing, and I can share*
> *Jesus with him. I can love him and calm him down.*

28

He needs me."

"He doesn't have any money because his ex-wife took it all, but I can help him get a better job and show him how to take care of his finances."

"He has low self-esteem, that's why he accuses me of things and doesn't want me to spend time with anyone else but him, but I can help him feel better about himself."

"He never calls me to tell me he's going to be late, but I'm sure he has a good reason."

"I know he doesn't read his Bible or go to church even though he says he's a Christian, but you know how men are."

There are many other lies we believe that get us into bad relationships, even marriages that were never God's will in the first place. This is what God wants us to avoid. It is His desire that we are equally yoked to our mates, not unequally yoked. The trouble in the flesh that we bring upon ourselves is so painful and unnecessary when we do things our own way. If we would simply listen to Him, let the Holy Spirit guide us, and not make decisions in haste based on our own selfish desires, we would spare ourselves a world of hurt and heartache down the road.

Don't get me wrong here. If you were unequally yoked when you got married, and are having trouble in your marriage now, YOUR MARRIAGE CAN BE BETTER! Just start with being real with yourself, work on you and God will begin healing those broken places. Have you ever been through the pain of divorce?

> *Emotionally and spiritually, it is much like death and despair. Imagine having your heart ripped from your chest and being without hope altogether. This is what it felt like to me. Imagine feeling these multiple times.*

Have you? I sincerely hope not. The damage can be debilitating for years to come, and can cause depression, anxiety, hopelessness, weight gain, physical ailments, and loss of faith. I experienced these, at different times. Divorce also deeply affects those you love, such as family members, friends, and co-workers. Many young and old today prefer to live together and refuse to marry because of the many failed marriages of others around them.

As Christians, people are always watching us to see how we respond when life gets difficult. They want and need to see God active in our lives. We cannot waste another day, another moment, drowning in our own sorrows! It's time for us to realize our worth in God's eyes.

The Psalmist King David wrote:

> *How precious and weighty also are Your thoughts*
> *to me, O God! How vast is the sum of them! If I*
> *could count them, they would be MORE in number*
> *than the sand, when I awake, I am still with you.*
> *(Psalm 139:17-18 AMP)*

Do you understand how many thoughts toward you that is? Think about the beach and how many grains it takes to make up just a small handful of sand. I got to thinking about this and decided to look up microscopic images of sand on the internet. I was awestruck to find the most breathtaking images of the most beautiful shapes and colors imaginable, and I encourage you to do the same. Not one of them is exactly alike. Think about this for a moment. If you don't yet understand, or, are still in the process of letting Jesus Christ and God the Father with the Holy Spirit be your Husband, then hold on, because the next chapters will encourage you to know who you are in Christ as his daughter, his bride, his beloved. He is not finished with you, and he will use you again if you are willing to believe.

> *And the Beloved of the Lord shall dwell in safety by*
> *him; He will cover him (her) all the day long. He*
> *dwells between his shoulders. (Deuteronomy 33:12*
> *KJV)*

Oswald Chambers, author of the book *My Utmost for His Highest* wrote:

> *"The way we continually talk about our own inabilities is an insult to our Creator. To complain over our incompetence is to accuse God falsely of having overlooked us. Get into the habit of examining from God's perspective those things that sound so humble to men. You will be amazed at how unbelievably inappropriate and disrespectful they are to Him. There is only one relationship that really matters, and that is your personal relationship to your personal Redeemer and Lord. If you maintain that at all costs, letting everything else go, God will fulfill His purpose through your life. One individual life may be of priceless value to God's purposes, and yours may be that life."*

2

Faith Erupts from a Dream

It happened with a dream. I had been hearing from the Lord and others for several years, "Terri, you should write a book for Christian women struggling with a history of divorce about how to heal and be made whole again!" Well…every time I heard that message there was another one, and another one immediately waiting behind it:

You can't write a book.

You're not an author.

You're just a nobody.

You don't have a degree.

You're not a speaker.

You don't have the resources, the time or the money. You're destitute. Nobody wants to hear what you have to say.

Your family hates you and wants nothing to do with you. You are a failure.

Even if you did write a book, it takes money to get it

published. Money, you don't have.

Even if your manuscript did reach the eyes of a publisher and they decided to read it, they wouldn't like it and it wouldn't be published.

Even if you found a publisher, no one would read it. It would just collect dust on the shelves.

And, even if it was published, sold and read, all your awful past will be exposed, and you'll be put to shame by all your readers."

Did you know that Satan is the father of lies? Let's look closely to what the Bible tells us about his lying nature:

Father of Lies

Ye are of your father the devil, and the lusts of your father ye will do. He was a murderer from the beginning, and abode not in the truth, because there is no truth in him. When he speaks a lie, he speaks of his own: for he is a liar, and the father of it. (John 8:44 KJV)

Designed to Undo God's Work

And these are they by the way side, where the word is sown; but when they have heard, Satan cometh immediately, and taketh away the word that was sown in their hearts. (Mark 4:15 KJV)

Deceiver in Character

And the great dragon was cast out, that old serpent, called the Devil, and Satan, <u>which deceives the whole world:</u> he was cast out into the earth, and his angels were cast out with him. (Revelation 12:9 KJV)

Insinuates Doubt

Now the serpent was more subtle and crafty than any living creature of the field which the Lord God had made. And he (Satan) said to the woman, Can it really be that God has said, You shall not eat from every tree of the garden? (Genesis 3:1 AMP)

Satan has spent his entire existence on mastering the art of lying. So, I kept ignoring the prodding from yes, the Holy Spirit to write this book until one divine morning. Just prior to that divine morning I had been lying on my face daily, crying out asking God to give me purpose, community, a good church home and a good job. I asked for good friends and money to survive after my fifth divorce. I woke up. It was 4:00 a.m. I began recounting the vivid dream I just had.

I was in a large building, very busy with people going in and out. It might have been a court building, or perhaps a bus or train station. I knew in my heart and had a strong sense that my husband was somewhere there. I felt this desperate longing to find him and be with him. The idea of finding him was almost euphoric in my dream – in a sense, it seemed like I was searching for the antidote for all my previous poisonous and injurious relationships.

Hastening from room to room I inquired to anyone who would listen, "Has anyone seen my husband?" only to be met with a deafening feeling of shame and disgust from everyone I encountered. An overwhelming, compulsive drive to press on in my search loomed as I just knew it would pay off in the long run.

My heart pounded, and tears flowed down my cheeks. I felt so alone. A sick feeling of rejection began to cover me like a dark heavy blanket. I felt swelling waves of fear and despair wash over me again and again.

Next, I came to a large room like a court room with masses of people standing in lines, against walls and sitting on cold metal benches waiting to be 'heard' by a judge or some kind of official. Then I heard my name called and was escorted into a room. There before the judge, I pleaded to find my husband. His response was harsh and demeaning. He pounded both his fists on the desk as if my plea was a complete waste of his time.

He yelled, "Your husband is not here and even if he was, he does not want to see you!"

Then two tall and strong security guards took me, arm in arm, and pushed me out of the room and onto the floor. I remember feeling completely abandoned, worthless and hopeless, and began to sob uncontrollably. I walked out of the building. Then I woke up. Still reeling over the sick feeling in my heart and mind from the dream, it occurred to me I did not know who the husband was I looked for, because I couldn't see his face in my dream. To date I've had five husbands and it was none of them. Bursting with curiosity I immediately asked God what this meant.

As I laid in bed, covers over my head in the dark as I often did, I felt like God was saying to me, "Terri, Terri, I'm right here! You've already found me. I've been here all along with you. I will never leave you or forsake you. Come with me. Come. I will satisfy you when you are sad. When you are thrilled about something I will listen and even talk to you. I will take you to places of victory and freedom, heights that cannot be touched with your physical understanding. I will make you whole again. You know this feeling my daughter. Come, let us go again!"

Then the words began pouring out of my heart about this dream, about this book I would write, and finally I was inspired by my husband, the lover of my soul Jesus Christ as I thought:

> *"Dare to Dream Terri for something bigger than*
> *you could ever imagine."*

He told me it was okay to believe large and expect the best. When the motives and intentions of my heart were to be that beautiful bride that wanted so desperately to be accepted, loved, validated, heard, and held,

I really and truly could do all things through Christ
who strengthened me. (Philippians 4:13)

In the first few months after my divorce from my fifth husband, I rented a room from a gracious English woman I'll call 'Grace'. She was so good to me and my sweet little 'Roxy girl', the absolute cutest Toy Fox Terrier Chihuahua mix known to man, and my gift from God for comfort and kisses. Grace also had a dog and welcomed us both into her quiet and safe abode.

It was perfect timing - Grace would be gone for the Thanksgiving holiday and Roxy and I would have the house to ourselves. Wondering what I was going to do for Thanksgiving, I began a mental list to see which opportunity would suit me best. My family was preparing the annual get-together, but the destination was further away than I wanted since I don't enjoy driving long distances alone. So, that was out. My parents lived nearby, but we recently had a rift, and I didn't want to deal with it, so, that was out. I thought about serving at a soup kitchen, but the closest one was forty minutes away. Again, not interested in the drive. That was out too.

I began to think this would be the perfect time to let God have his way with me, face my fears, and start weaning myself off anti-depressant drugs that I had taken for fourteen years. I decided to fast and pray, work on Christmas projects, and write this book. I knew a book couldn't be written in five days, but I chose to dream big! In between writing chapters for the book and Christmas projects, the Lord told me to write a love letter to myself and it went something like this:

Dear Terri,

I love you! Listen to this wisdom:

After three glasses of wine your clear thinking will be gone. You will lose the ability to make sound choices. You will put yourself in harm's way. You may over-eat and feel things that you wouldn't while sober. You will imagine things that are not real, and you will be vulnerable.

Wine is a mocker; strong drink is raging: and whosoever is deceived thereby is NOT wise. (Proverbs 20:1 KJV)

Who hath woe? Who hath sorrow? Who hath contentions? Who hath babbling? Who hath wounds without cause? Who hath redness of eyes? They that tarry (remain or stay) long at the wine; they that go to seek mixed wine. Look not thou upon the wine when it is red, when it giveth his colour in the cup, when it moveth itself aright. At the last it biteth like a serpent, and stingeth like an adder (venomous snake). Thine eyes shall behold strange women, and thine heart shall utter perverse things. Yea, thou shalt be as he that lieth down in the midst of the sea, or as he that lieth upon the top of a mast.

(WHAT... TRY TO PICTURE THAT!!!).

They have stricken (afflicted with disease, trouble or sorrow) me, shalt thou say, and I was not sick; they have beaten me, and I felt it not; when shall I awake? I will seek it yet again. (Proverbs 23:29-35 KJV)

Then there's tomorrow Terri! You will be hung over and feel incredible guilt. You will feel sick and have heart palpitations because your body is weak. You will feel afraid because you have disappointed your loving Lord again. You know the scriptures, and you will know you have been willfully disobedient.

Don't hate yourself Terri just because other people reject you. Think about them and why. You are not what other people say you are. Remember your value and worth Terri. Remember who you are, who your husband is and how much he loves you. You will get through this Terri. Let it run its course. It's a good thing that you feel this way. You were not meant to be alone. You can work through this loss Terri with Jesus' help. Stay the course this time Terri.

You can do all things through Christ who strengthens you. (Philippians 4:13)

People who have hurt you and alcohol can't make you feel better or give you what you need. You don't need to keep putting yourself in harm's way. Find good people and start good healthy relationships Terri. Love yourself the way God does. Treat yourself fairly and with respect. Feed yourself healthy foods. Get what you need to care for your own basic necessities.

This time Terri, be happy with yourself, so you can reflect His love to others who need it."

I pray that you will be inspired to write a love letter to yourself. Be truthful. Don't leave anything out. It may mean going to the dark and difficult truth. Only you know what you need to tell yourself to begin your own healing journey.

God also told me to write down things about me that were positive, strengths, things I admired about myself, and my greatest accomplishments. He reminded me that instead of getting angry when I made mistakes it was good to laugh, and to continue making others laugh, it's how He made me and makes Him happy to see me happy. You can do this too! You will find yourself loving yourself again the way God wants you to. He does! He died on the cross for you. That kind of love is unfathomable, but true. Please believe it.

Thus, began the unfolding of my story of healing and deliverance.

> *I was endowed with courage and strength from the love I've been searching for all my life, Jesus Christ.*

I believe God inspired me to write this book to encourage you, and to expose Satan's lies meant to perpetuate the bondage of bad relationships and divorce. I want to encourage you to fall in love with the man of your dreams, Jesus Christ, and realize how much He loves and values you as His daughter, His Precious Bride, His beautiful creation.

> **You can make good decisions, and, dream big again!**

3

Knight #1

Lost in Love

We were just two teenagers in love. I'll call him Knight#1. My best friend invited me to a nearby party and there he was……..with long curly locks of blonde hair, and the most beautiful tan I had ever seen. He was your typical 'surfer dude'. He was dancing with another girl who was very beautiful. Immediately I felt flushed and embarrassed for my staring at them both. A few moments later he came over to me and asked me to dance. I thought for sure I would die right there in his arms. I can still hear the Beach Boys singing "Girl Surfer Girl, My Little Surfer Girl". I fell head over heels in love, and from that night on we dated for four years.

We enjoyed trips to the beach and cruising the streets in his gold Chevy Impala station wagon. The attention he gave me was intoxicating, and I would do anything to be with him.

> *I was blinded by my own desires and didn't realize the devastation soon to come. Spurned by early childhood rejection and abandonment, I was about to make harmful decisions that would change my life forever.*

I began walking three miles from my house to his, taking almost an hour every morning before school. I left at 6:00 a.m. and would quietly slip in his front door and into his bed. Afterwards, he would drop me off at school and I was thrilled to show him off to all my friends.

Proudly I hand sewed thick yellow and orange curtains to go all around the windows of the Chevy station wagon, so we could be alone. Unfortunately, we were alone more than we should have been. We would frequent secluded places to be intimate and I willfully gave away the precious gift of my virginity. Sex with him was the most exciting thing I had ever experienced in my life. We were inseparable.

Eventually, my mom caught onto this and she took me to the local clinic to get a prescription for birth control pills. After starting the regimen of birth control my menstrual cycles suddenly changed and were extremely heavy, painful and debilitating. I often missed school due to the discomfort.

A few months later, guess what? I was pregnant.

I wouldn't have known because I had my regular cycle, but I had sharp shooting pains on my right side and dizziness, so my parents took me to the hospital. The doctor said I had an ectopic pregnancy where the fetus implants itself outside the uterus inside the fallopian tube. Ectopic pregnancies can be serious if the fallopian tube ruptures,

44

as it could result in internal bleeding and infection. I was given methotrexate to miscarry and spent the night in the hospital. This was a painful and traumatic experience.

As time went on, I got pregnant again. I felt devastated and confused. I often dreamed of my blissful future marriage to my 'Surfer in Shining Armor', but we began to grow apart. Jealousy took root, mixed with immaturity and a dysfunctional upbringing, eventually chipped away at our tender love for each other. Now in a tornado of guilt, rejection and abandonment, I thought abortion was the answer. My parents agreed so they took me to have the procedure done at a local hospital sometime in 1973. This was just the beginning of a downward spiral on the slippery slope of false love.

I continued to date my surfer dude because I thought our love would last, besides, he already gave me an engagement ring, and I was convinced we would marry eventually. I craved marriage and love so much but was painfully unaware of the immaturity and brokenness in both our young lives.

Three years later I was pregnant again with his child. I was on birth control ladies. It doesn't always work. Trust me. I told him I was pregnant, but jealousy again reared its ugly head.

I was now three months pregnant, alone and scared. Knight #1 wasn't convinced the child was

his. I was crushed and angry (or at least that's the
way I chose to remember it).

The way I saw it, I gave this young man my whole heart and he stomped on it! Again, early childhood issues of rejection and abandonment at work caused us both to believe lies about each other. But thank God, years later would bring about truth and forgiveness between us, and a true relationship between Father and Son.

I thought I was not capable of raising a child on my own but was opposed to the idea of another abortion, so I considered adoption. I went to a few meetings at a local adoption agency, but as I got further and further along in my pregnancy, I realized how much I loved this child growing inside me and could not bear the thought of giving him to someone else. He moved and stretched in my belly especially when I sang to him and I couldn't wait to meet him.

I was freshly out of high school and still lived at home. Thank God my parents loved me and were an integral part of my decision to parent. Mom took me to Lamaze birthing classes and was my birthing coach. I got the support I needed to care for myself and my child during my entire pregnancy. This was such a blessing.

My son was born after 26 hours of hard natural labor, and moments after his initial wipe down by the nurse, my active little blonde-haired, blue-eyed jaundice baby boy promptly grabbed the side rail of his incubator and wouldn't let go!

As an infant, he was colicky and didn't sleep well. As a toddler, he was everywhere all the time, on the go. His blonde locks and blue eyes attracted everyone around him, and he was such a Ham!

There I was, a single Mom with no experience and not off to a good start. I did my best as a single mom, but my best was broken and bruised!

I worked full-time for the General Telephone Company in Santa Fe Springs, California as an administrative assistant but struggled financially. Determined to save money, I foolhardily jumped at a multi-roommate situation. It was not a good environment. In fact, it was a monumentally life-changing disaster! I willingly, and without conviction found myself in a willing deluge of drugs, alcohol, and more men.

> *I felt my life spinning out of control. It was not a*
> *good environment for me and my son.*

Sometime during this crazy spin-cycle of life, my sister gave her life to the Lord and began sharing Jesus with me every chance she could get. I was pretty annoyed every time she brought up 'Jesus' and would do my best to avoid conversations with her.

One afternoon, for no apparent reason at all and completely

unannounced, she came over to my apartment, and I was.........

'Not in a good place' in the other room. She patiently waited for me to come out and when I did, she excitedly invited me to a Phil Keaggy Christian concert at Cerritos College that very night. She appeared completely oblivious to my wayward surroundings and just let her boldness for the Lord fly! At first, I declined, as I did every other opportunity she presented to attend a Christian event, but she was particularly persistent on this day. I was taken by her notable and strange compassion and was somehow convinced to attend. Holy Ghost and God's love drawing me all the way!

To make a long story short, I went, I heard!

> *The Holy Spirit got a hold of me and I could not get down to the football field fast enough to give my wretched, stinky, life, over to a God I could not see, and wasn't even sure I believed in at all!*

I was so ready to shake loose the ugly shackles that kept me bound to a lifestyle I hated. I so desperately wanted to be loved.

I did it! I asked the Lord Jesus Christ into my life to be my Lord and Savior and to wash me clean from all my sins. I plainly told him I didn't even know if he was real, but if he was, could he please do something with this ugly life of mine. I must have cried for days.

Then I walked on clouds for what felt like the next three or four months and began sharing Jesus with everyone I knew, boldly and with amazing zeal. Many of my friends, co-workers and total strangers gave their lives to the Lord back then. As I shared my new-found peace and contentment, they saw a dramatic change in my demeanor and lifestyle. I felt so relieved of my heavy burdens of sin. I felt clean again! And had hope like nothing I had ever experienced even as a child.

> *Then, right on schedule came Knight #2 and Knight #3, ergo the song, Lookin' for Love in all the wrong places!*

Look up the lyrics of that sweet old song we all know too well. Can you relate to those lyrics, or do you know someone else who can? Wow! Ever notice how songs have a way of helping to shape our thoughts and actions? Think about that for a moment, and we'll revisit it later in the book. I didn't realize until too late in life how I willingly let the secular songs of my day mold and shape my way of thinking in my search for true love. What a mistake! I'll discuss how to avoid this in a further chapter.

In contrast, it helps to surround yourself with true believers in Christ who live for Him and have a life that reflects that relationship. I didn't realize how important it was and didn't recognize what a true believer really looked like. I needed someone to show me these things, but for whatever reason, I didn't make it a priority.

*I was so focused on the outward appearance and negative attention that I simply could not see clearly to make the best choices. Though I loved the Lord Jesus, **He wasn't Lord of my life yet**. My understanding and thought processes needed to be changed, this would take time and more heartache before I would truly begin to make better decisions. Thank God that's not the end of this story!*

Sanctification is a journey. God is compassionate and patient with this process concerning us, his creation. He proved this on the cross, and we can fully trust Him through the days, months, even years of relentless and tiresome efforts to clean ourselves up. He completes the work in us, and we come to understand His truth.

4

Knights #2 and #3
A Downward Spiral

Well on my way as a dysfunctional single parent at age nineteen and living back at home (again the love and grace of my parents), it was time to find a husband to take care of me and my son. Right? Another lie adopted. Another mess created. Down I went!

Though I had a good job and a safe living environment with my parents to help me raise my young son, I had already begun to fill my life's shopping cart with plenty of baggage, abandonment, and rejection issues. My patience level was around zero to five at best. My loving sister, wanting to help me out of a difficult situation, introduced me to a colleague she thought might be a good match for me, Knight #2. Oh boy. What a mistake!

I wasn't at all attracted to this person physically or emotionally when we first met. In fact, he was stoic, and stood confidently gazing what seemed to be right through me. I remember feeling both scared and safe at the same time. He was well dressed and appeared to be financially stable with his fancy watch and nice car. I was solely attracted to these reasonable attributes, and so made up my mind that

I would go for him as he showed an interest in me. What was I thinking? Obviously, I was not thinking clearly at all, but I can see now where my thinking was warped by my goal to 'find a husband' at all costs.

This was my chance to have some stability, to give my three-year-old son a father, and to have a future. I leaned completely on my own understanding and the wisdom of the world. Yikes! I didn't think to ask God if he was the right one, because I didn't know the Lord yet. I only 'thought' I knew him. But still, He was not #1.

Oh too shortly after my son's fourth birthday we got married. A few years later we had a baby boy. Quite the opposite of his brother, he wanted to be born right away. He was an emergency C-section, and four hours later he was wrapped comfortably like a 'glow worm' in a blue and white hospital receiving blanket. He was calm and quiet and beautiful. He slept through the night as a newborn, and as a toddler he rarely got into mischief. If we ever did have to scold him, he would pucker his lips with a sad face and cry. We nicknamed him "Kootz".

His big brother took good care of him, helping to feed him and change him, and they were inseparable.

We owned a home, had good jobs, made good money and didn't lack any comforts, but our lives were total chaos. I did not know this until after we were married, but my second husband was involved with the mafia, did drugs, smoked marijuana and frequented the bars.

Sometimes he stayed out all night without calling and would come home drunk and disheveled. We argued over this often and our relationship became volatile.

During this, my second marriage, I was bringing others to Christ and was 'on fire' for God. We attended a local church and had a good circle of friends. I wanted everyone to know this Jesus the way I did. At the same time, I had such a deep longing to know Jesus in his fullness, and to understand more about the Holy Spirit and walking in victory, healing, and blessing. Also, I cried out to God constantly to change my circumstances and save my husband.

I was baptized with the Holy Ghost and received the gift of tongues in my bathtub one night simply by asking for it. I found great comfort in spending time praying in the spirit and being immersed in God's peace. Wild, child-like faith kept me hungry for more of God during this difficult phase of my life.

Apart from my husband, my sons and I experienced many miracles and healings as we exercised our faith, we were growing spiritually as a family in 'leaps and bounds'.

One night my oldest son was running around the house and I shouted "Stop running. You're gonna hurt yourself." Sure enough, as the words left my lips, BAM! He hit a wall, hard, and then started screaming! I ran to pick him up off the floor and his forehead had already started forming a 'goose egg'. I picked him up and laid him on our bed. By that time, the goose egg was red and the size of a golf ball.

> *At that moment, I heard the Lord say to me clear as a bell, "Okay Terri, now is the time for you to seek me and receive healing for your son by standing on the scriptures I gave you." I immediately laid my hand on my son's forehead while he was screaming and quoted Mark 11:23-24*

> *Whatsoever things you desire, when you pray, believe that you have received them, and you shall have them.*

I asked Jesus to heal my son, and as I did, I felt a warm tingling sensation go through my arm, and down my hand and fingers.

Immediately the goose egg on his forehead disappeared. I was amazed and humbled and started to cry. God met me right where my faith was in that moment. My son sat up on the bed with a shocked and astonished look on his face. I told him that the Lord just healed him, and he should go look in the mirror. He felt his forehead and looked shocked as he anxiously jumped off the bed and ran to the full-length mirror in the hallway closet. In innocent astonishment, he saw the bump was gone. He dropped to his knees and with a beautiful, sweet quivering voice said, "Thank you Jesus!" Neither of us have forgotten that day, it was truly amazing. And the devil can never take that away. Never!!!

From then on, I tried desperately to change my husband into a Christian and get him to behave, but unfortunately, it didn't work. Our life together seemed to intensify in violence and anger the more I prayed. I did some of the goofiest things in those days like laying on the floor for hours in the form of a cross on my face. I fasted and prayed, cried, and screamed. You name it. I did it! I walked with God for two years, but when the bottom finally dropped out of my life, I immediately blamed him and walked away. It was never His fault, just me making hasty decisions without asking Him first what He wanted for me. Not yet knowing Him completely as my Lord and my Love.

After suffering five years of violence, and physical and verbal abuse, my baggage was overflowing as I grew more and more angry with each passing day.

I recall one Saturday afternoon we were at a local park for a barbeque with my husband's family. After drinking beer all afternoon, my husband, Knight #2 accused me of flirting with another man. He started yelling at me in front of everyone. I turned to walk away from him, and he began to chase me, fast.

> *I ran as fast as I could, but he caught me and threw me down on the ground. Then he grabbed my hair in the back of my head and pulled a fistful of hair from my head and said, "You will never get away from me. Never!" I was crying in spasms of shock, my ears were ringing, and I was bleeding.*

It took several months before the hair began to grow back in the bald spot left on my head. There were other violent attacks. One of the worst occurred one day at home when he again accused me of being unfaithful. When I yelled back at him to deny his claim, he threw me down on the living room floor. I was in a sitting position with my legs extended in front of me when he jumped on my back, on his feet with his full weight, he crushed my back. It took a full year of chiropractic treatments before I could return to a normal lifestyle.

In addition to the physical abuse, there was sexual and verbal abuse.

We were married a little over a year when he told me it was okay, even normal for a husband to use profanity and pain during sexual intercourse. He told me that it was okay if it was just between us, and that it was healthy for our sex life. About a year later I had reconstructive surgery performed on my reproductive system to repair tissue damage. I was afraid of him, and even more afraid to tell anyone about the abuse. He often threatened to kill me. My young sons were also subjected to his sudden verbal and physical outbursts. I believe it has left deep scars in them both to this day.

We divorced in 1988 and I was, ergo the song, 'Alone again, naturally'. Fueled by anger I began a downward spiral of drugs, alcohol, and endless empty relationships. I had hardened my heart at this point beyond reasoning and was out of control. Looking back, I remember a sermon my pastor preached several years later that very appropriately describes what can happen to the heart. These were my own notes:

Anger is not unrighteous in itself, but we need to

work these things out in our lives. Your flesh can erupt like a volcano at any time and the hot lava just hardens all over, nothing can grow around that for a <u>very</u> <u>long</u> <u>time</u>. We are fooling ourselves that we are even a Christian if we continually behave this way. Calm down!! People lose their cool because they never get control over their emotions. Even Solomon lost his cool continually because his heart wasn't right. Anger can be an addiction. There is never an excuse to lose control. Anger produces fruit. It is a selfish problem. We don't get to use any excuses as to why we lose control, i.e., someone else's actions or lack of.

Some months later I met Knight #3 at a club and brought him home with me. The following week he moved in with me and said,

"Hey, why don't we get married? If it doesn't work out, we can just get a divorce?" How about that? In my bitterness, I said, "Sure. Why not!" In late 1991, we were married before the justice of the peace.

"Without restraint, bitterness can cause a total destruction in a life that does not love and fear God but craves to satisfy only its own selfish desires."

We divorced a short 6 months later in early 1992. I was numb at this point and did not care about much of anything, nor the consequences I would suffer later.

I tried to hold on to some semblance of Christianity but sank deeper and deeper into my own bitterness. I willfully slipped into darkness, doing and saying, the abominable. I was bitter but afraid, because I knew I was out from under the shadow of God's protective wings. That was the year of a devastating California earthquake in my very own hometown of Whittier. I remember coming home right after the quake to find my home in shambles. It literally looked like someone had picked it up like a doll house, turned it upside down and shook it violently, leaving everything thrown onto the floor and broken to pieces. I was scared to death and felt like God's judgment had fallen on me for my wrong doings. I felt strong conviction that I could not shake.

I had been working for a large phone company for eight years and in 1992 decided to go into business for myself - anything to make a drastic change in my life, so I didn't go crazy. Meanwhile, I had repented of my sins and started going back to church. I read my Bible and tried to get close to God again. Feeling both mental and physical effects of the sting of sin in my life, it was difficult to come crawling back to Jesus. Daily I fought a tremendous sense of numbness and hopelessness. I had no idea that I was still trying to put a man, another human being first before Jesus as my true love. I did not realize He was the one I could have put first.

> *I still deeply longed for the true love of an honest man in my life. I wanted it all more than anything - the white picket fence, a nice home, and a happy family. This was my goal, above all. I couldn't imagine anything else and continued to make this my highest priority no matter what. It continually gnawed at my heart like a tormenting melody. I had no idea it would come at such a high cost.*

5

Knight #4
All that Glitters Is Not Gold

Earlier I mentioned that I had gone into business for myself after a career with the phone company. I met a woman I'll call 'Marge'. She was a cosmetic consultant and did her best to recruit me. She eventually won me over as I sought yet another path to success.

I was eager to start something fresh after Knight #3, and I began to do in-home facials and makeup with Marge. I really loved this kind of work, and not having to work for someone else. I was ready to take on the world!

A few months later, Marge came to me with a proposition for a consulting position she recently accepted at a local medical center. Marge had a background in management, particularly in the medical field. She asked me if I would be interested in working with her to install and manage a new inventory system and to oversee three other departments. It would take one to two years in a contract position. The compensation was exceptional and so were the benefits. I would work directly under her as my supervisor, but we would be in full control of the entire project.

I had a background in information technology, administration and inventory control, this was right up my alley. I accepted, and we went straight to work building the new empire.

The first thing we did was hire our team. I was responsible for interviewing and hiring new warehouse workers who could start right away with the inventory process. For the hospital industry, this was a huge undertaking, and a slow and tedious operation. We had to inventory over 4,000 basic hospital medical supplies and pieces of equipment to start. We also did a different inventory for the operating room with all its different sizes of screws, catheters, and bandages. Then there were the items we would add because of a brand-new state-of-the-art inventory system. I needed to hire fast.

Knight #4 came in for his interview and was right on time with a firm handshake and the most stunning smile I had ever seen. I was taken instantly by his adorable face and especially that 'smile'.

I tried hard to be professional and to act like I didn't think he was cute at all, so I turned up the 'stuck up, stuck on myself' attitude to thwart any possible attention to my instant attraction to this beautiful young man.

We all began to work very long hours, inventorying, inventorying, inventorying. Marge and I were up all hours of the night for weeks on end getting every single item put onto inventory sheets for the company who would build our database.

I found a new purpose in life and was feeling good about myself and my outward appearance. I was in great shape because I worked out at the gym twice a week and felt attractive and self-confident. I spent a good amount of money on professional business outfits that were extremely high-class and provocative. This gave me a sense of control and self-worth, and I liked it a lot! Tough as nails. That was my image.

Ladies, I'm trying to paint a picture here. This type of mentality can get you into a lot of trouble, a lot of trouble! It did me.

> *I began to act like the 'Cougar' as this young man was twelve years younger than me. Yes, you heard me correctly. Twelve years. I was thirty-one and he was....you guessed it, nineteen.*

He was a hard worker, extremely pleasant to look at, and willing to work extra hours to get the inventory finished. Knight #4 was also eager to learn more about purchasing and had a very professional attitude.

There was an instant magnetic attraction between us as we worked long hours and got to know each other on a personal level. Well......long story short, we were in a relationship quickly. We began to spend time together outside of work, and he fell in love with my two boys and they loved him.

Somewhere along the line, I quit spending time with Jesus and going to church because now I was on my way and obviously didn't think I needed Him. All was well, and I was too busy working and being a single mom. I was sure God would understand.

The first six months or so of the relationship was pure excitement and a complete 'oxytocin fix'. I had this one wrapped around my finger, and I knew it. I was having fun controlling my world and not looking to him as husband material. Over time though, a year or so, I was beginning to really 'fall in love' with this young man. My defenses came down and my heart became soft and vulnerable again. Oh no! He was gorgeous and sweet, great with my sons, and we got along so well. We decided to move in together.

About a year later, we were one happy family living together when he told me his parents were moving to Seattle, Washington. He wanted us all to move there so we could have a better life.

We began to weigh the pros and cons and quickly concluded the move was a good decision. It was beautiful, and the economy was better. It was close to the water and had a lower crime rate and cost of living. I concluded it wasn't that far away from my family and immediately sprang into action to make it happen!

Another goal I had was to get my youngest son away from his father, Knight #2. He was abusive to us all and he threatened to kill me on several occasions if I ever left him. I wanted us all as far away from him as possible.

My Knight #4 made the move before us to pave the way ahead while the boys and I wrapped things up at home in California. I had two garage sales, and a few months later we were ready to move. We found a place right away and began our new life. Knight #4 was working for a bank, and I began a career with the school district as an administrative assistant. We lived together as one happy family. Right?

> *Immediately upon arrival to our new home I fought a year-long custody battle for my youngest son. At the end, I lost the court case and was devastated to learn that his abusive father would have primary custody.*

I did, however, get joint custody with three months during the summer break, alternating birthdays and holidays, and every other weekend I could afford to fly him home.

Soon after the custody battle ended, we settled down nicely in our new home in Seattle and I decided it was time to find a church. I found one nearby, and we all went that following Sunday. Well, did we find a church or what? This church was everything I wanted - small, non-denominational, casual, Bible believing, spirit-filled, and very welcoming. I went down to the altar for prayer and rededicated my life to Jesus. I learned later that when they gave the altar call, started talking in tongues, and laying hands on each other, Knight #4…was looking for the door.

When we got home after the service, I told him I needed to talk to him about something serious. I said I was a Christian who needed to live for Jesus and would be making some changes in how I lived my life. I also told him that I could not live with him anymore and that we were unequally yoked. I said I wanted to get married and that he needed to be a Christian. That was the only way I could stay with him.

He replied, "I will do whatever you want and become a Christian, because I don't want to be without you!"

He said he was raised Catholic, and that his parents would be very upset about his marrying a Christian and converting, but he didn't care because he loved and wanted me.

Can you see here how I was manipulating my own circumstances to get what I wanted? My own understanding got me into this mess because I could validate it all day long to seem like the right thing, because…I wanted it so badly.

Winter of 1992, amidst the painfully cold, rain, snow and ice, our new church family gave us a warm and sweet wedding. With an abundance of gifts and more love than we could have hoped for, we hopped on to the ride of marital bliss. We began what seemed like the perfect little Christian family journey. We went to church every Sunday and Wednesday, had revivals during the week, and were busy living our faith. Eventually we became the youth leaders of the church. We lead youth group events, counseled, and baptized the youth. We also started a band, a drama team, and an evangelism team.

Often, we would visit our sister churches in other cities to support their evangelistic efforts in their communities. Helping others and acting in a place of authority was somewhat addicting. It felt so good to have close friends and to share our spiritual lives in the Lord. Unfortunately, neither of us had the deep-rooted relationship with Jesus that was so needful for what was about to happen.

It seemed rather suddenly that we had been married ten-and-a-half years. We argued all the time over money and just about everything. I realize now that I never seriously considered his age nor his faith before we married, but still expected him to be the spiritual leader of our family. Our differences in age and experience made conflict resolution nearly impossible.

We went to counseling but our marriage was devastated by roadblocks of preconceived expectations on so many levels that a path to a healthy marriage seemed impossible.

Sometime later, in a desperate attempt to save our marriage, we decided together to move to Texas as my husband took a transfer with his job, looking yet again for a fresh start. Why Texas, you ask? Why not? He worked in retail and his regional manager told him there was another store that needed help in another state. There is much more to the real story as to why Texas, but I choose to lean on the side of grace and forgiveness, as God does with us, so, have left out those details. My oldest son was an adult and on his own, and my youngest son could visit us anywhere. This was my validation thinking. We needed to start fresh somewhere just the two of us I thought. Another lie. I would have done just about anything to save this marriage. I even went as far as getting my naval pierced just to keep him attracted to me. I was desperate to try just about anything.

We were in Texas for one fleeting summer when things began to quickly unravel at the seams. Suspicion and intolerance gave way. With my list of offenses and a broken heart I left him to return to our previous home and church family in Seattle.

This was truly the most devastating time of my life. I was so in love with this man that I could not see straight, literally. I was completely blinded by what I wanted, the perfect husband. This just could not be happening. I tried to hold our marriage together by praying and pleading, and he eventually came back to us in Seattle. We reconciled for about three months, only to find it was too late, the marriage was dead, I had to let go.

Amazingly, something precious was inserted into this tragic time warp. For some reason, he went to the animal shelter and found a small miracle. A redheaded Chihuahua, Papillion, toy fox terrier mix puppy who had gone astray. He brought her home to me, and she became my new companion, my sweet gift from God. I named her Roxy. I see now how God was always watching over me, and He knew I would need this little love to get me through the coming days.

About four months later he moved out and we agreed to divorce. The arguing, and being unequally yoked, finally took its toll.

Marriage #3, and the dream of the perfect life was over in January of 2002 after ten years of marriage.

On top of that our beloved pastor recently moved to Africa and the church dynamic drastically changed. I felt a tremendous sense of failure and loss and wondered what to do next. There was only one thing that made sense. Go back home to California to be closer to family. After a month or so of planning and saying Goodbye to our precious church family and friends, Roxy and I made our way back to California.

Completely and utterly numb at this point my reasoning tank was on empty. I wasn't angry at God, I was just numb and couldn't think straight. I wasn't seeking God to this point for wisdom either. I just didn't care anymore. I was so desperate for the love of a man.

Let me paint a quick picture of my relationship with Knight #4. I found an art term called 'Alla Prima' on the web site "essentialvermeer.com" that best describes how it started.

Alla Prima is an Italian term meaning "at first attempt." It indicates a method of oil painting in which a picture is completed by painting on the entire surface of the canvas all at once rather than by traditional method which required a methodical building of the image, piecemeal fashion with successive layers of paint. Today, Alla Prima painting is generally referred to as direct painting. In French, it is called premier coup.

In a sense, I painted this relationship 'all at once'. I could have used the more traditional method by waiting on God and building the image with more success, but instead, I chose the more compulsive route based on my own understanding and the picture was complete. Following a certain method, usually produces typical results.

Think about the popular song sung in the 1939 film The Wizard of Oz, "If I only had a Brain", also "If I Only Had a Heart" and "If I Only Had the Nerve". I took the easy way out because I wanted it 'Now'. I tried to force the relationship to be something it wasn't. The age difference of twelve years, and not sharing the same faith were major factors in the death of this marriage. If I had only waited on God and asked Him what to look for in a spouse instead of running off like the cowardly lion, the canvas of my life could have been so different. But God uses everything. Nothing was wasted. And hope was on the horizon!

> *And we know that all things work together for good to them that love God, to them who are the called according to his purpose. (Romans 8:28 KJV)*

6
Knight #5
From 'On the Rebound' To 'Waking Up'

I found work right away as a caregiver for a home health agency and a nice roommate situation with a dear woman in Anaheim, close to Disneyland. After returning from Seattle spending time with my family was a priority, but I often felt like the black sheep, and was haunted by feelings of loneliness and rejection. I just wanted the pain to stop. So…I got on Match.com. What??????

> *No joke. Less than three months from arriving back*
> *in California I met Knight #5.*

He was gentle, had an intriguing career in the movie industry, and was a pilot, which I found to be too interesting. Unfortunately, alcohol was a strong bond between us, Oh and Jesus of course. How about that?

Not so funny, but after dating for a few short months, he also said to me "Why don't we get married. If it doesn't work out, we'll just get a divorce."

Uh oh! I hear an echo from Knight #3 in Chapter Four. Guess what? In July of 2002, we married after only three short months of dating. Bet you didn't see that one coming, did you? Okay, another lie I believed. But then again, I didn't care, so I went for it. Wouldn't you think I would have had an epiphany or something? Nope! Blinded by my own desire for love I headed right into the fire once again. He was nice, was a Christian, but I ignored the rebound state that silenced clarity and wisdom. We married so quickly I did not see the hidden issues that would surface in the short future.

Can you say, "Molotov Cocktail"? Listen to this perfect definition by Wikipedia to describe this relationship:

A Molotov cocktail (Finnish: Polttopullo or Molotovin koktaili), also known as a petrol bomb, bottle bomb, poor man's grenade, fire bomb (not to be confused with an actual fire bomb) or just Molotov, is a generic name used for a variety of bottle-based improvised incendiary weapons. Due to the relative ease of production, Molotov cocktails have been used by street criminals, protesters, rioters, gangsters, urban guerrillas, terrorists, irregular soldiers, or even regular soldiers short on equivalent military-issue weapons. They are primarily intended to set targets ablaze rather than obliterate them.

Trust me on this, the enemy of your soul can handcraft the perfect destructive relationship for you every time. All you must do is turn a blind-eye, and poof! Up-in-smoke you go.

We enjoyed trips around Southern California and cooking, cooking was one of his passions. He taught me how to prepare and enjoy foods I'd never tried before with a concentration on healthy alternatives. I learned how to cook fresh food with a variety of herbs and spices and became quite a food entrepreneur. Everything with lots and lots of garlic and red onion - you can never go wrong. I can speak of these things now, with a bit of 'tongue and cheek' because I know I am forgiven, and my sins are washed away by the Precious Blood of the Lamb. I choose to celebrate the good from my life's experiences and am grateful for the Lord's work and patience through His grace and mercy. You can too!

We attended his church nearby, which I enjoyed, until he told me that many in the church didn't think it wrong to drink wine, and lots of it. This was a problem for me because alcohol has been a problem for me since childhood. When I drank, my mind went astray, for example: I recall a time when my father tucked me in bed after a party, he was drunk. He kissed me on my ear, and the way he smelled and sounded made me sick. Godly examples, teaching and support were important to me, red flags were popping up, but God was still at work.

Knight #5 frequently had parties with fancy meals for church friends and his inner circle. We prayed and talked about God a lot at these parties and even counseled each other. Unfortunately, I would often drink too much wine.

One good thing came out of the church we were attending, a class was offered about dysfunctional relationships and codependency. I took the eight-week course and learned so much about myself. This helped me add tools to my toolbox for major repairs I would need to make along the path to healing, just ahead.

Our marriage lasted almost one-and-a-half years. Amazing. Does this all sound crazy to you? Well, it was. Now that I have found the one true love of my life, it is hard to believe I was so willingly deceived in my own thoughts, but I was. I did not recognize or use sound wisdom, because I didn't ask the one who mattered most, Jesus Christ.

At this point, I was the dysfunctional one. I admit it. I realized when Knight #5 asked me to leave his house and wanted a divorce, I couldn't trust my own thoughts anymore!

Who was I? One messed up woman. I felt like ending my life. How could I let this happen? How could I be so stupid? I must be crazy! I didn't like me at all. I figured that it was my fault that all these relationships ended because of me. I reasoned I was a terrible human being to make them want to leave me. I started to believe that I would never make good choices again and that my life would always be a tragedy.

I nearly completely lost all hope of any happiness in my life as I struggled to get out of bed and to be positive in any way. I started drinking again to ease the pain.

I think he knew how broken we both were, and what a terrible mix this was. He knew I needed help, but he couldn't help me because of his own issues. Knowing this he quickly filed for divorce and gave me money to be on my way. I didn't believe he meant me any harm, and so we wished each other well as best we could and amicably parted ways. This was in 2004.

I was not able to work because I was anxious and sad and hopeless all the time, I was depressed. I eventually succumbed to the fact that I needed to see a therapist. I had to talk to a professional, or I was not going to make it. I found a therapist and started weekly sessions. I was having regular panic attacks, so the therapist put me on anti-depressants. This helped, and I was grateful for the temporary relief it brought. I still didn't trust my own thoughts and was scared to death for the first time in my life for my future, and for the future of my now adult sons who were also deeply affected by these relationships. But seeing the therapist regularly was one of the best things I ever did for myself.

In the depths of my despair, dashed hopes and seemingly a total destruction of mind and heart, I must have cried every day for what felt like months on end. It was truly the darkest time of my life. I was just beginning to wake up to reality and realize when and where I had made bad choices. So, started my healing journey. It was a long one, but at least it was started. As the old saying goes: Start small. End big, but just Start!

Meanwhile, the sister who brought me to the Lord lived nearby and graciously let me rent a small room attached to her garage. One night while drowning in my sea of sorrow I drank a whole bottle of wine. While I lay in my twin bed crying to the Lord, I told him I wanted to die. I told him I couldn't live with these scars anymore. I wanted to know why all this tragedy had happened to me. I told Him I did not want to be alone, plain and simple. But if I was meant to be alone, I wanted to be happy. I begged God to bring a man into my life once and for all before I was too old. I asked Him to let the man love Jesus first. Then I asked Him to let the man be old fashioned like my dad, and I asked Him to let the man love me for who I am. I cried and cried and cried that night curled up against the wall on my twin bed.

My little Roxy girl cleaned up more tears during these days and kept me on my toes to keep me moving because she needed me! By the way ladies, it helps to have a dog. I highly recommend finding one with a sweet temperament and one that loves to be held. For me it was a positive distraction. Roxy brought me so much unconditional love. She helped keep my mind occupied on positive things when it started to veer off in a negative direction. I thanked God that he brought this little pup into my life. She was a very special gift.

7

Knight #6
The Beginning of the End

It was a warm and glowing Sunday morning in the quaint little bed and breakfast town of Sierra Madre, California. I was going to church no matter what - no matter what I looked like, no matter what I felt like, and no matter how late I would be. I only wanted to hear from God and to seek His face. I didn't want to make another mistake: this was my new goal. So, I put on my muumuu to purposely avoid bringing any attention to myself in church, slipped on some sandals and flew out the door.

I was probably fifteen minutes late walking through the church doors when, yup, you guessed it - Knight #6, an usher no less, approached me to help me find a seat. Much to my surprise the open seat just happened to be right next to him. Imagine that! I listened to the sermon and thought to myself how boring and watered down the message was. I was also turned off by how morbidly obese the pastor was and was distracted by how much he sweat while he preached. Funny, the things our minds retain. I wondered if I should come back or look for another church. As I listened to the sermon, I felt God tell me to stay put and keep coming to this church until he told me otherwise.

I met a sweet older couple that Sunday who took an interest in me and invited me to dinner at their home nearby. I accepted. Meanwhile, as I was getting ready to leave, Knight #6 approached me with his business card in hand. He told me he was a financial consultant of sorts and asked me to call him if I could use his services. What? Did I look like a total flake deadbeat who needed his services, or was he just trying to pick me up? Are you kidding me? What a salesman! That was a total turn-off for sure. What a slug, I thought! I only attended the church a few times and had absolutely no desire whatsoever to call this financial consultant for any services, that was for sure!

Several weeks later I was on my way to getting my act together and looking to make better decisions all around, including my finances. I decided to run my credit report and quickly discovered I could probably use this guy's services after all. I hesitatingly called him and asked if he could help me with my credit. He said he'd take a look at my report and let me know. I made an appointment to meet with him at a nearby restaurant a few days later.

He was already waiting at a table outside of this quaint little curbside restaurant when I arrived. I said hello and promptly handed him my credit report. I sat down, and he quickly read it and informed me that he couldn't help me. He said my credit needed a lot of work. It would be expensive, and he couldn't guarantee the derogatory items would be removed or that my credit score would improve. Not what I wanted to hear at all, but I wasn't surprised. All I could hear was another shame-based message that offered no hope. He then explained how I could begin cleaning the report myself. It would be a long and arduous process, but it could be done. I felt somewhat relieved that I could eventually call myself a responsible human being again, but to be honest, I really wanted a 'quick fix' and was immediately disappointed.

We continued to talk for a bit, and the conversation went well. We were enjoying each other's company. He suggested we share some dinner, and we went into the restaurant where he ordered a steak cut-up into bite size pieces with toothpicks. He said it was easier to eat, we could maintain eye contact, and I didn't have to be concerned about finesse. Also, people are generally more comfortable with finger foods, he added. Clever, I thought, very clever! We went on talking for hours about life in general, and even touched on what we both wanted in a marriage. We made lists on the paper placemats at our table and then compared them. Much to my amazement and suspicion, they were remarkably close.

This meeting became what I call our first 'non-date'. He asked if we could see each other again and I said, "I'm not interested in dating right now." I told him I was very recently divorced and did not want to make another mistake.

He said, "Okay, maybe we could just spend time together as friends, non-dating." Reluctantly, I agreed.

We began to non-date almost every day thereafter. We spoke on the phone often and sat together at church.

We non-dated for about a week or so, then we were full on dating. We talked about everything. He sent flowers to my work and wrote me sweet playful notes that brought a smile to my face. One time he sent me flowers with a note from Miss Roxy, telling me she was happy, and she looked forward to us all moving in together. She was in love with him, and he with her. He took me out to dinner and bought me clothes. Oh, his license plate read: "DNT QUIT". I thought that was unique and maybe a good sign.

It was obvious to me that he was much more engaged in our relationship than I was. Sometimes I felt bad that I wasn't as affectionate as he. I tried explaining the deep sense of numbness I felt from past failed relationships and that I wanted to move slowly. He didn't seem the least bit annoyed or moved by any of this, and his refreshing compassion encouraged me. He told me that he was there for the long-haul and would peel back the onion one layer at a time to help me recover the lost affection and emotions. I began to think it may be worth hanging in there just to see what he would do next.

At first, I shared my past relationships with him, but as we grew closer, I began to share some of my dark and shameful past that haunted me continually. These were the sins of the past that God was fully aware of when I bowed my heart to him, for which he had already forgiven me. These sins were washed away clean by his own precious blood that He willingly and knowingly shed for me on the cross. He did this for you too!

Then I heard a loud voice in heaven, saying, "Now the salvation, and the power, and the kingdom (dominion, reign) of our God, and the authority of His Christ have come; for the accuser of our [believing] brothers and sisters has been thrown down [at last], he who accuses them and keeps bringing charges [of sinful behavior] against them before our God day and night. (Revelation 12:10 AMP)

It is because of the Lord's loving kindnesses that we are not consumed, Because His [tender] compassions never fail. They are new every morning; Great and beyond measure is Your faithfulness. (Lamentations 3:22-23 AMP)

As far as the east is from the west, so far hath he removed our transgressions from us. (Psalm 103:12 AMP)

Do you know the story in the Bible of the adulterous woman? This is what Jesus thought of her. Let this truth seize your mind and your heart:

But Jesus went to the Mount of Olives. Early in the morning He came back into the temple [court], and all the people were coming to Him. He sat down and began teaching them. Now the scribes and Pharisees brought a woman who had been caught in adultery. They made her stand in the center of the court, and they said to Him, "Teacher, this woman has been caught in the very act of adultery. Now in the Law Moses commanded us to stone such women [to death]. So, what do You say [to do with her—what is Your sentence]?" They said this to test Him, hoping that they would have grounds for accusing Him. But Jesus stooped down and began writing on the ground with His finger. However, when they persisted in questioning Him, He straightened up and said, "He who is without [any] sin among you, let him be the first to throw a stone at her." Then He stooped down again and started writing on the ground. They listened [to His reply], and they began to go out one by one, starting with the oldest ones, until He was left alone, with the woman [standing there before Him] in the center of the court. Straightening up, Jesus said to her, "Woman, where are they? Did no one condemn you?" She answered, "No one, Lord!" And Jesus said, "I do not condemn you either. Go.

From now on sin no more." (John 8:1-11 AMP)

See, we have no excuse to let the devil beat us up with thoughts of shame that simply are not true. If we listen long enough to his lies, we can start to believe them. Don't! Kick him out immediately. Put him on notice:

Casting down imaginations, and every high thing that exalteth itself against the knowledge of God, and bringing into captivity every thought to the obedience of Christ. (II Corinthians 10:5 KJV)

Commit thy works unto the LORD*, and thy thoughts shall be established. (Proverbs 16:3 KJV)*

Oh, did I tell you that Knight #6 was a New-Yorker, with the accent and attitude to boot? Well, there were plenty of times when he would say or do something that I thought was completely rude, and it probably was, but to him, it wasn't. This guy was the king of sarcasm and it was hard to take, often. With the baggage of rejection and abandonment in one hand, and fear and insecurity in the other, there were more than a few explosions that occurred between us as we got more and more comfortable in our relationship.

Regardless of all that, we decided to move in together strictly as roommates, not lovers. Uh huh!

With all the fiery defense and intent that this redhead could muster, and with finger pointed in the air, I often told my Knight that there would be no sex, but he would have to marry me if he wanted to pursue a permanent relationship. Twelve times he asked me to marry him and twelve times I said "Yes." We married in June of 2004 about 3 months later in front of the justice of the peace in Norwalk, California. The ceremony was conducted by a precious woman with weighty words like 'commitment, and covenant'. I was surprised and deeply humbled by her words which I will not soon forget. We had two wonderful witnesses at the ceremony, my youngest son, and Wayne's long-time good friend. We were pronounced Mr. and Mrs. and he told me right then and there, and often over the years, that he would be my last husband.

We moved around from church to church and maintained a good old lukewarm relationship with the Lord that lulled us into a somewhat justified state of consciousness. I knew in my heart-of-hearts that I still had not made Jesus first even then. We would have times of good fellowship, but brokenness often led to drunkenness and arguing.

Fast forwarding through the next eight years, we enjoyed great strides of growing in the Lord, falling back, good success in business, losing our jobs, great health, near-death experiences, and tragic loss. We clung as best we could to the Lord and experienced many undeserved miracles of provision and healing all along the way. But, at the same time, selfishness, fear, anger, and doubt gave way to the erosion of trust in each other. Exhaustive efforts on both our parts to hold our marriage together finally took their toll. I, with all my baggage and need for the perfect Christian husband to fix my life, decided our marriage was over. I believed my Wayne was deceptive and mean. I had hatred in my heart towards him and held him responsible for the death of our marriage, and maybe unknowingly, every hurt I ever had. He was no angel, and I had plenty of reasons to want out, but concluded we were unequally yoked. This was my validation to quit. We agreed to divorce and went our separate ways in 2012.

So, began the process of what I believe to be true redemption in both of our hearts. Whenever I share the redemptive story of our reconciliation, I often say that God said, "Okay Terri, you over here to the left, and Wayne, you over here to the right, we have a lot of work to do in the both of you!"

I quickly went to work trying to get my little Christian world all together, so I could in some way feel good about myself again. Boy, did I have a lot to learn?

In my desperation for answers, the Lord quickly took me to another set of sermon notes in the back of my Bible that helped anchor my soul and my emotions from completely going sideways, here they are:

The <u>Sovereignty of God is GREATER than the power of discouraging circumstances.</u> When God speaks, it is a divine covenant in which we can rest. It is a divine covenant which <u>ACTUALLY</u>

ENABLES US to rest in the Lord for a POSITIVE AND FINAL OUTCOME for those things that did not turn out the way we think they should, the way we think they could, or even the way we prayed. The Lord can overrule your prayer anytime He wants to.

You can pray one way, but God sometimes moves another way. But when He does, He always ends up fulfilling His promise one way or another. Maybe not the way we want, but the way His sovereign authority chose to. This is the basis for sweet surrender. True Love, True Healing, and True Peace comes from true surrender to God. Stay with me as a real-life story unfolds.

8

Declaring My Soul to Believe
and My Enemy to Leave

The first year after my divorce from Wayne was a fierce and emotional roller coaster, since to date, I had never been without a man in my life. Learning how to let Jesus be my all-in-all took me thirty years after becoming a Christian. Aside from having babies, it was one of the hardest things for me to do without running headlong into yet another bad relationship. I want to be sorely honest here, so hopefully you won't waste as many years as I did before the light bulb 'goes on'!

I can't tell you the countless times I would get in my car late at night and drive to the local fast food restaurant for a taco, a shake, or some other comfort food to hopefully drive away the intense longing for the emptiness inside. The thought of my body being the temple of the Holy Spirit was always there, but I chose to ignore it. I used to cringe at the thought of what my arteries looked like after eating fast food nearly every day for one full year. Yikes!

Do you not know that your body is the temple (the
very sanctuary) of the Holy Spirit Who lives within

you, whom you have received (as a Gift) from God? You are not your own. You were bought with a price (purchased with a 'preciousness' and paid for, made HIS OWN). So then, honor God and bring glory to Him in your body. (I Corinthians 6:19-20 AMP)

Each day I fell prey to the thoughts of guilt and shame over five failed marriages and couldn't seem to get out from under that heavy burden of hopelessness. I was reminded constantly of my failure to be a decent human being. I couldn't stop thinking about the fact that I was divorced for the fifth time! How I would never be pure again. I felt used up, damaged goods. I kept thinking that I was the woman that every mom would tell her son to watch out for, to stay away from! Oh, but I was quickly reminded by my Lord of the following story in the Bible.

The Samaritan Woman at the Well

Then a woman from Samaria came to draw water. Jesus said to her, "Give Me a drink"— For His disciples had gone off into the city to buy food— The Samaritan woman asked Him, "How is it that You, being a Jew, ask me, a Samaritan woman, for a drink?" (For Jews have nothing to do with Samaritans.) Jesus answered her, "If you knew [about] God's gift [of eternal life], and who it is who says, 'Give Me a drink,' you would have asked Him [instead], and He would have given you living water (eternal life)." She said to Him, "Sir, you have nothing to draw with [no bucket and rope] and the well is deep. Where then do You get that living water? Are You greater than our father Jacob, who gave us the well, and who used to drink from it himself, and his sons and his cattle also?" Jesus answered her, "Everyone who drinks this water will be thirsty again. But whoever drinks the water that I give him will never be thirsty again. But the water that I give him will become in him a spring of water [satisfying his thirst for God] welling up [continually flowing, bubbling within him] to eternal life."

The woman said to Him, "Sir, give me this water, so that I will not get thirsty nor [have to continually] come all the way here to draw." At this, Jesus said, "Go, call your husband and come back." The woman answered, "I do not have a husband." Jesus said to her, "You have correctly said, 'I do not have a husband'; for you have had five husbands, and the man you are now living with is not your husband. You have said this truthfully." The woman said to Him, "Sir, I see that You are a prophet. Our fathers worshiped on this mountain, but you Jews say that the place where one ought to worship is in Jerusalem [at the temple]." Jesus replied, "Woman, believe Me, a time is coming [when God's kingdom comes] when you will worship the Father neither on this mountain nor in Jerusalem. You [Samaritans] do not know what you worship; we [Jews] do know what we worship, for salvation is from the Jews. But a time is coming and is already here when the true worshipers will worship the Father in spirit [from the heart, the inner self] and in truth; for the Father seeks such people to be His worshipers. God is spirit [the Source of life, yet invisible to mankind], and those who worship Him must worship in spirit and truth." The woman said to Him, "I know that Messiah is coming (He who is called Christ—the Anointed); when that One comes, He will tell us everything [we need to know]." Jesus said to her, "I who speak to you, am He (the Messiah)."

Just then His disciples came, and they were surprised to find Him talking with a woman. However, no one said, "What are You asking about?" or, "Why are You talking to her?" Then the woman left her water jar, and went into the city and began telling the people, "Come, see a man who told me all the things that I have done! Can this be the Christ (the Messiah, the Anointed)?" So, the people left the city and were coming to Him. (John 4:7-30 AMP)

Here is what the Lord spoke to me about his visit with the Samaritan woman.

First off, he took the time to 'talk with her'. How about that? He knew full well what she had done in her life, and he did not shame her by using words that were demeaning or offensive.

She took the initiative and straight out asked him why he was asking her for a drink when it was culturally unacceptable in those days for a Jew to speak to a Samaritan, let alone a woman. Wow. Talk about bold. Jesus, being God himself, could have shamed her just for her boldness, but he didn't. Instead he began to tell her about the gift of eternal life. That's compassion.

Jesus told her about her past marriages and how she was now living with a man, but still, he did not shame her. He continued to have a matter-of-fact conversation with her and stuck to the facts. Salvation.

The Samaritan woman immediately left all her things at the well and began to evangelize. How awesome is that? Jesus knew what she was going to do after he took the time to let her know the truth.

The same goes for us. It's TRUE! Let Him use you to touch the lives of others. He knows who you are and what you are all about. He didn't miss anything. He laid down His life for you and is not ashamed of you in any shape or form.

> *But God hath chosen the foolish things of the world to confound the wise; and God hath chosen the weak things of the world to confound the things which are mighty. (I Corinthians 1:27 KJV)*

After my divorce, I also took up drinking, again! It started with a glass of wine here and there, and then there and here and back again. Before I knew it, I was up to a whole bottle by myself when I was having a tough time. I struggled with this for several months. Typically, the weekends were the hardest. I would agonize over my convictions and the hangovers, repent, return to my vomit, repent, and return to my vomit again, until I finally had enough and cried out to Jesus for strength. This gross picture is meant to warn and teach us, but we don't get a clue until it's too late. If you've ever watched a dog do this, it's wincingly repulsive, disgusting, and a picture of what we should avoid!

> *Like a dog that returns to his vomit Is a fool who repeats his foolishness. (Proverbs 26:11 AMP)*

On top of all that, I was in full-blown menopause! Hormones every which way and loose; gained thirty extra pounds; and got the worst haircut in my life (of which I'm certain I still haven't recovered). I was not happy with me at all! I knew I was trading one addiction for another and would continue down this road until I finally gave in and let Jesus take control.

My hope is that this book helps you on your own journey to making Jesus your all-in-all, once and for all, replacing destructive thinking, behaviors, and relationships. It wasn't easy, but here's what I did.

First, I realized I needed to go to the Lord, be open, and ask for strength to stay the course. I had to stand on His Word! Without these four simple truths, I was doomed for sure in my own strength.

> *"Lean on, trust in, and be confident in the Lord with all your heart and mind and do not rely on your own insight or understanding. In all your ways know, recognize, and acknowledge Him, and He will direct and make straight and plain your*

paths." (Proverbs 3:5-6 AMP)

"But He said to me, My grace (My favor and loving-kindness and mercy) is enough for you (sufficient against any danger and enables you to bear the trouble manfully); for My strength and power are made perfect (fulfilled and completed) and show themselves most effective in (your) weakness. Therefore, I will all the more gladly glory in my weaknesses and infirmities, that the strength and power of Christ (the Messiah) may rest (yes, may pitch a tent over and dwell) UPON ME"! (II Corinthians 9:9 AMP)

Hallelujah. This is great news! Once I really let this truth sink in, I got it! I realized that it was a done deal, and I didn't have to struggle or suffer anymore. He said it, I believed it, and that settled it! And guess what? It worked. How about that! Of course, we all have our own journey, and we all need to be comfortable in our own skin it's true, but there is something about *Believing* what the scriptures plainly speak to us. It becomes real for you, and that is where the personal husband relationship with Jesus begins to unfold.

Second, I began to leave messages to myself on my smart phone that sounded something like this:

"Okay Terri. This is sound wisdom. Listen to this message every day and ask yourself if it's worth it. Is it worth it to go buy a bottle of wine, for the moment? Is it worth it to experience what you're going to feel afterward? You'll wake up in the middle of the night, hungover; you'll repent again; you'll feel terrible physically, spiritually and emotionally. Think about why you want to drink. Is it because of (name the man or the issue)? Is it because you're desperately lonely, or what? Is it worth it? It's not Terri! Count the cost, ahead of time. Catch yourself. Think about this Terri. Be good to yourself. Love yourself enough to say no. You can say no! It's easier to say no than to say yes and then have to deal with how you're going to feel later. Are you willing to disappoint the only man in your life that's ever truly loved you? Is it worth it to disappoint Him Terri? Think about how good you will feel afterward because you said no. You can do this Terri.

"He who the Son sets free IS FREE INDEED."
(John 8:36 KJV)

Once and for all Terri Lynne, love yourself enough to say no!"

Using my first name and speaking to myself with my own voice made it personal. This was important to me as I was not getting much 'good attention' from others, and I knew that this was my journey, and no one was going to make me better but me. Once I laid hold of the

95

fact that I needed to 'take action' for myself, that God loved me enough to reveal to me how much He loved me through His Word, I decided to take that action, and to put into practice these revelations for my own healing.

Third, I put another message on my smart phone, a warning. It went something like this:

"Okay Terri. Here we go again. It's (I put in the date so I could see my progress). You drank a whole bottle of wine last night because (name it i.e., you broke up with.... or whatever your own struggle is/was). On top of that Terri, you got in your car, under the influence, and drove into town to get something to eat. Terri Lynne, you're gonna get killed. You're gonna get pulled over and thrown in jail. Do you want that at (I put in my age)? Do you want that? You have got to count the cost Terri! Stop this! Stop it now!"

That's just an example. But each one of us knows what our issues are, and we're fully aware when we commit willful sin, especially if we have the conviction of the Holy Spirit. *We have got to be faced with the brutal truth of ourselves before change comes true.* Here is a scripture the Lord gave me as a warning that I would never heal unless I brought to Him what ailed me and dealt with it:

> *Hear, O heavens, and give ear, O earth! For the Lord has spoken: I have nourished and brought up sons (and daughters) and have made them great*

and exalted, but they have rebelled against Me and broken away from Me. The ox (instinctively) knows his owner, and the donkey his master's crib, but Israel does not know or recognize Me (as Lord, as Husband) My people (daughter's) do not consider or understand. Ah, sinful nation, a people loaded with iniquity, offspring of evildoers, sons (daughter's) who deal corruptly! They have forsaken the Lord, they have despised and shown contempt and provoked the Holy One of Israel to anger they have become utterly estranged (alienated, divorced). Why should you be stricken and punished any more (since it brings no correction)? You will revolt more and more. The whole head is sick, and the whole heart is faint (feeble, sick, and nauseated). From the sole of the foot even to the head there is no soundness or health in (the nation's body) – but wounds and bruises and fresh and bleeding stripes; they have not been pressed out and closed up or bound up or softened with oil (No one has troubled to seek a remedy). (Isaiah 1:5-6 AMP)

This scripture not only captured my whole heart and soul but helped me realize how much He was speaking to me personally. The scripture stirred up a stronger reverence and healthy fear of God in my life. Remember this one:

> *Kiss the Son (pay reverence to Him in purity), lest He be angry and you perish in the way, for soon shall His wrath be kindled. O blessed, (happy, fortunate, and to be envied) are all those who seek refuge (shelter or protection from danger) and put their trust in Him. (Psalm 2:12 AMP)*

Let's face it. We all want to be loved. We have it deeply rooted in us to have a Person in our lives that will treat us with respect, sensitivity, and compassion. Yes, this is the way He created you, to desire this so deeply. A man who will romance us, shower us with gifts, have long talks and listen to us. Right? We even long for this man to have authority over us and take control when we are having a meltdown. Truth be told, we deeply wish this man to be gentle, yet bold and strong at the same time, which can often lead to a twisted and unbalanced relationship if we don't let the mind of Christ lead us in wisdom.

Fourth, I began to ask myself what I needed and what was missing by not having a man in my life: The things I missed about being married and how I could put Jesus in those missing places. So, I began to talk to Him when I was alone, all the time, as if I was talking to 'my husband'. Whether I was tired, rested, sore, energetic, lonely, happy, angry, content, confused, acting wisely, desperate and calm, I began to sense His presence as never before. Though it helped having my sweet companion Roxy, the cutest little redheaded Chihuahua toy fox terrier mix ever created, she still took a back seat to the Lord in my life.

I used to dread thinking about the weekends all alone and fearing I would fall desperately on my face once again. But now, I look forward to my weekends with Him. I love my alone time with Him in the morning over coffee. I love my worship, His Word, His promptings. It's important to have ample time to listen to Him speak to me and not do all the talking. He is always ready for long talks, is sensitive to my needs, and is faithful to fulfill my deepest longing for love. No, He's not a genie in a bottle, but He does hear our prayers and longs to spend time with me, with us.

I am always amazed but not shocked at how God is constantly working in my life. At any time, I can ask Him for help, and He is always available to give me what I need, even when I don't get an answer right away. He only asks me to do what is right and He will make a way for me, even when I blow it.

And the Lord said to Cain, why are you angry? And
why do you look sad and depressed and dejected?

If you do well, will you not be accepted? And if you do not do well, sin crouches at your door; its desire is for you, but you must master it. (Genesis 4:6-7 AMP)

Just as Cain, we too can just do what is right and God will take care of us. We have been given all we need. We just need to realize it and believe it.

Our journeys are all different, and we all learn at different times and seasons the perfect will of God. But if we simply 'show up' He will show himself faithful.

Here are some of His encouraging words that spoke to me during my darkest days and nights. They helped me be conscious of His presence in my life:

Let be, and be still, and know (recognize and understand) that I am God. I will be exalted among the nations! I will be exalted in the earth! The Lord of Hosts is with us; the God of Jacob is our Refuge (our High Tower and Stronghold). Selah (pause, and calmly think of that) (Psalm 46:10-11 AMP)

Fear not, for you shall not be ashamed; neither be confounded and depressed, for you shall not be put to shame. For you shall forget the shame of your youth, and you shall not (seriously) remember the reproach of your widowhood any more. For your Maker is your Husband – the Lord of hosts is His name – and the holy One of Israel is your Redeemer; the God of the whole earth He is called. For the Lord has called you like a woman forsaken, grieved in spirit, and heartsore – even a wife (wooed and won) in youth, when she is (later) refused and scorned, says your God. (Isaiah 54:4-6 AMP)

He took me to these scriptures. Gave me permission, and told me to stand on His Word, and to **Declare My SOUL TO BELIEVE and My ENEMY TO LEAVE!** It is our inheritance to be victorious, but we must actively *believe.*

But no weapon that is formed against you shall prosper, and every tongue that shall rise against you in judgment you shall show to be in the wrong. This (peace, righteousness, security, triumph over opposition) is the heritage of the servants of the Lord (those in whom the ideal Servant of the Lord is reproduced); this is the righteousness or the vindication which they obtain from Me (this is that which I impart to them as their justification), says the Lord. (Isaiah 54:17 AMP)

101

*For I know the thoughts and plans that I have for
you, says the Lord, thoughts and plans for welfare
and peace and not for evil, to give you hope in your
final outcome. Then you will call upon Me, and you
will come and pray to Me, and I will hear and heed
you. Then you will seek Me, inquire for, and
require Me (as a vital necessity) and find me when
you search for Me with all your heart. I will be
found by you, says the Lord, and I will release you
from captivity and gather you from all the nations
and all the places to which I have driven you, says
the Lord, and I will bring you back to the place from
which I caused you to be carried away captive.
(Jeremiah 29:11-14 AMP)*

Too often we think someone, or something, will fulfill our lives
with happiness and true peace. But too often they do not, and we
continue our journey to find that fulfillment utilizing whatever means
necessary. Wisdom and understanding seem to fail when things begin
to fall apart, or we don't get our way. These powerful words, once
they became real to me, delivered me from continued torment and
hopelessness.

*For no temptation (no trial regarded as enticing to
sin, no matter how it comes or where it leads) has
overtaken you and laid hold on you that is not*

102

common to man (that is, no temptation or trial has come to you that is beyond human resistance and that is not adjusted and adapted and belonging to human experience, and such as man can bear). But God is faithful (to His Word and to His compassionate nature), and he (can be trusted) not to let you be tempted and tried and assayed beyond your ability and strength of resistance and power to endure, but with the temptation He will (always) also provide the way out (the means of escape to a landing place), that you may be capable and strong and powerful to bear up under it patiently. (I Corinthians 10:13 AMP)

Rejoice in the lord always (delight, gladden yourselves in Him); again I say, Rejoice! Let all men know and perceive and recognize your unselfishness (your considerateness, your forbearing spirit), The lord is near (He is coming soon). Do not fret or have any anxiety about anything, but in every circumstance and in everything, by prayer and petition (definite requests), with thanksgiving, continue to make your wants known to God And God's peace (shall be yours, that tranquil state of a soul assured of its salvation through Christ, and so fearing nothing from God and being content with its earthly lot of whatever sort that is, that peace) which transcends all understanding shall garrison and mount guard over your hearts and minds in Christ Jesus. (Philippians 4:4-7 AMP)

For the rest, brethren, whatever is true, whatever is worthy of reverence and is honorable and seemly, whatever is just, whatever is pure, whatever is lovely and lovable, whatever is kind and winsome and gracious, if there is any virtue and excellence, if there is anything worthy of praise, think on and weigh and take account of these things (fix your minds on them). Practice what you have learned and received and heard and seen in me, and model your way of living on it, and the God of peace (of untroubled, undisturbed well-being) will be with you. (Philippians 4:8-9 AMP)

Let's recount the steps I took that worked for me and if necessary, see if you can find something that works for you.

STEP 1:

a) Realize and be aware that you need, and can go to, the Lord.

b) Be open, willing, and honest with yourself and Him.

c) Ask Him for His strength to stay the course.

d) Ask Him to give you scriptures that will minister to you specifically and stand on His Word. Write them down anywhere and everywhere. Without these four simple truths, you may be doomed for sure in your own strength.

STEP: 2: Leave messages to yourself to 'Catch Yourself' before you make a bad decision. I used my smart phone, and then listened to myself in my own confrontational voice speaking to me about the truth. It's amazing how we can justify what we want no matter what. But we can clearly see, with eyes wide-open and acutely aware, how to be better equipped to change our minds for a better future.

STEP 3: Warn yourself. If STEP 2 isn't enough and you know it isn't, then remind yourself of the danger ahead. Don't be afraid to be graphic. Remember, this is just for you alone. Be specific about what God has protected you from so far and stir up some healthy fear that reminds you of the last time you went head on into dangerous territory. Maybe caution yourself regarding someone else's fate due to a bad decision. You can describe the details better than anyone and know exactly what it will take to get your attention. If you are willing, the Lord will help guard you from another defeat.

STEP 4: Ask yourself what you think you are missing and what you need. This may take some time and real effort to fully examine and understand yourself. You may need to ask God to reveal this to you. Once you grasp these, you can recognize when and where the triggers are. Then you can begin to put Jesus into these needs. Example: I was lonely and felt sad that I did not have a husband and I was alone. So, I began to speak to Jesus as my husband every day and went to Him for all the things I thought I needed in a husband. Does that make sense? I hope so. It is a realization that took some work, but as I went to Him daily to replace the things I thought I needed, I began to experience the joy of overcoming. Wow!

I believe the biggest mistake I made in my life so far was not being honest with myself. I continually chose to fend off looking at myself in the mirror and admitting to my own faults. Once I finally chose to honestly examine my own heart and actions, I was able to see so much clearer and then make better decisions. It was, and still is, positively simple when you think about it.

> *The one true love of our lives only asks that we come as we are, with a willing heart, to take the first step.*

Another thing the Lord wanted me to share in this book is an important key element about identity. I don't know about you, and I think only the gals can truly relate to this, but, when I was about to be married, I nearly obsessed over my soon-to-be new last name. I began writing my whole new name repeatedly just to see what it looked like, how it sounded. It was fun and exciting! Somehow, I felt a sense of worth, belonging and identity, and even a fresh start in life.

Unfortunately, after my divorce to Wayne, failed marriage number five, I returned to my maiden name once more. I was devastated. I felt no identity at all. Divorce had swallowed me whole with no way of escape. Fortunately, and thank God, He gave me this scripture about my true identity:

> *He that hath an ear, let him hear what the Spirit saith unto the churches; To him that overcometh will I give to eat of the hidden manna, and will give him a white stone, and in the stone a new name written, which no man knoweth saving he that receiveth it. (Revelation 2:17 KJV)*

> *Come now, and let us reason together, saith the LORD: though your sins be as scarlet, they shall be as white as snow; though they be red like crimson, they shall be as wool. (Isaiah 1:18 KJV)*

This is the *True Identity* and future in Christ I had to look forward to, and simply needed to **Declare My SOUL TO BELIEVE and My ENEMY TO LEAVE!** The same goes for you my friend.

I remember a vision that the Lord gave me one afternoon after my divorce to Knight #4, Husband #3. I was seeking the Lord in prayer when he gave me a vision while I was awake. I prayed in the Spirit for over an hour and was 'caught up' in Him when I saw myself standing on a round pillar, only the width of my two feet together. It was completely dark all around me and nothing but empty space. I felt like I couldn't breathe. I knew the Lord was there and felt His presence but was so afraid of falling. Just then, he reached out His hand and said, "Take the first step Terri by faith, and when you do, I will carry you." I had to take the first step knowing there was nothing to step onto, just empty space.

Then I awoke from the vision. I marveled at this and was completely aware that God had given me this vision. I realized I must trust Him no matter what things looked like.

The Holy Spirit will always bring things to our remembrance. All we must do is ask him.

> *But the Comforter, which is the Holy Ghost, whom the Father will send in my name, he shall teach you all things, and bring all things to your remembrance, whatsoever I have said unto you. (John 14:26 KJV)*

I was reminded of this vision often during the first few years of my healing journey, and it encouraged me to stay the course no matter what. I love the way the Lord speaks to me when I am listening.

I didn't have any special answers or details about what I should do next, but I had a sense that all would be well if I just did what was right. If I was honest with myself. I was on the road to healing and I knew it. Praise God!

One day my little Roxy girl and I were walking through our little town where I was looking for work that would bring glory to God and meet my financial needs. I looked up and saw a sign that read "Pregnancy Resource Center". "Huh," I thought. "I wonder what that is!" Roxy and I went in and talked with the Executive Director and we three hit it off right away. This was a non-profit center where women who had experienced an unplanned pregnancy could learn about their options as alternatives to abortion. They offered free resources such as parenting classes, a baby boutique, baby furniture and other supplies. The director offered me a job and I ended up working there for four years.

Miss Roxy was a regular at the center and the clients often held her in their laps. It was a win-win for everyone. Clients, their children, and little Miss Roxy all received some extra needed love, acceptance, and comfort. Who woulda thunk. Right?

What I enjoyed most about my job was being a client advocate. I received extensive training on how to provide resources and help women see their value through God's eyes. While there, God gave me a wonderful circle of friends and support. My own sense of value and worth slowly returned as I too began to realize God's love. For this I am eternally grateful.

I am still amazed today how God just met all my needs. I didn't have to fret about anything. Everything fell into place as I put my trust in Him. I believe, as I did my part by going to church, spending daily time with Him in the Word, working my job, giving my tithe, and just doing the mundane tasks of everyday life, the Lord took special care of me. Here are the anchors for my personal beliefs:

...not forsaking our meeting together [as believers for worship and instruction], as is the habit of some, but encouraging one another; and all the more [faithfully] as you see the day [of Christ's return] approaching. (Hebrews 10:25 KJV)

This book of the law shall not depart out of thy mouth; but thou shalt meditate therein day and night, that thou mayest observe to do according to all that is written therein: for then thou shalt make thy way prosperous, and then thou shalt have good success. (Joshua 1:8 KJV.

So then faith cometh by hearing, and hearing by the word of God. (Romans 10:17 KJV)

Your word is a lamp to my feet And a light to my path. (Psalm 119:105 AMP.

My son, keep thy father's commandment, and forsake not the law of thy mother: Bind them continually upon thine heart, and tie them about thy neck. When thou goest, it shall lead thee; when thou sleepest, it shall keep thee; and when thou awakest, it shall talk with thee. For the commandment is a lamp; and the law is light; and reproofs of instruction are the way of life. (Proverbs 6:20-23 KJV)

And let the [gracious] favor of the Lord our God be on us; Confirm for us the work of our hands Yes, confirm the work of our hands. (Psalm 90:17 AMP)

Bring ye all the tithes into the storehouse, that there may be meat in mine house, and prove me now herewith, saith the LORD of hosts, if I will not open you the windows of heaven, and pour you out a blessing, that there shall not be room enough to receive it. And I will rebuke the devourer for your sakes, and he shall not destroy the fruits of your ground; neither shall your vine cast her fruit before the time in the field, saith the LORD of hosts. And all nations shall call you blessed: for ye shall be a delightsome land, saith the LORD of hosts. (Malachi 3:10-12 KJV)

But seek ye first the kingdom of God, and his righteousness; and all these things shall be added unto you. (Matthew 6:33 KJV)

But my God shall supply all your need according to his riches in glory by Christ Jesus. (Philippians 4:19 KJV)

You might recall that earlier in chapter two I mentioned a beautiful English woman I called 'Grace' whom I rented a room from? Well, she became one of my sweetest friends and a great encourager. We shared meals and long talks together. Sometimes we just hung out doing nothing more than petting our dogs. I felt so safe and at peace in her home. Grace had a next-door neighbor I'll call 'Sunny' because she had a smile that could light up a room. No kidding! No if's, and's, or but's about it, this gal was always there for good counsel and friendship. The three of us cooked, shopped, ran errands, and attended local events together. It was fun. If ever I was having a bad day, either of these sweet gals would stop and listen. A hug and a good word could instantly lighten my heart. I want you to see how God provided me with beautiful and sweet little gifts all along my journey. At the time, I didn't feel I deserved them. It was simply His love towards me. For that I am so grateful. These two women are still, and always will be, dear to my heart and highly valued friends that I can trust.

Almost two years after my divorce from Wayne in 2012, I was enjoying my job, church, and life knowing the Lord was by my side. I felt a strong sense of community and that the Lord was pleased with me. This is what I had always longed for but not realized. I had the true peace of God in my heart that I had struggled to attain my whole life.

I finally began to know Jesus as the husband I had always longed for. The Peace of God came from knowing Him, and believing Him, no matter what came my way. This kind of peace is not realized by many people today. Sometimes, this peace can be challenged by the devil who will try and rob us of it by throwing us a curveball. Maybe it shows up as cancer, a job loss, death, losing our home, theft, a divorce, or all the above. Or maybe someone's response feels like a personal rejection or attack, thereby triggering a wave of negative emotions. ***Whatever the strategy the devil uses, God's true peace is our portion as his kids, and can always be ours but we must seek it with every fiber of our being, and especially when we don't feel like it.***

> *And <u>LET</u> (keyword) the peace of God <u>RULE</u> in your hearts, to the which also ye are called in one body; and be ye thankful. (Colossians 3:15 KJV)*

> *Peace I leave with you, my peace I give unto you: not as the world giveth, give I unto you. <u>Let not</u> (keyword) your heart be troubled, neither let it be afraid. (John 14:27 KJV)*

Remember, **Declare Your SOUL TO BELIEVE and Your ENEMY TO LEAVE!**

This is not a mantra or some mind over matter way of thinking. *It is faith in action in God and His Word alone.* Bring your flesh and your thoughts into submission to the truth of the Word of God. Align yourself with the Word only. Be aware of your thoughts throughout each day. Take authority over negative thoughts immediately, before they have a chance to take root and steer you in the wrong direction.

> *So, submit to [the authority of] God. Resist the devil [stand firm against him] and he will flee from you. (James 4:7 AMP)*

> *He that hath no rule over his own spirit is like a city that is broken down, and without walls. (Proverbs 25:28 KJV)*

Last, but not least, I mentioned back in chapter three we would discuss how to avoid the negative messages in the secular songs of our day. How to avoid their powerful influence on our hearts and minds. One of the areas that God shined a bright light on for me, was the songs I listened to. As soon as I began to confront myself with the very habits, decisions, and thought processes that got me into trouble in the first place, God showed me, like playing back a video of the things I needed to know. The songs played over and over in my head.

Word for negative word their messages rang through my mind. I tried desperately to make them stop, but they would not 'give up the ghost' so to speak. It was literally tormenting. God showed me specifically that I needed to stay with the songs that lifted my heart, encouraged me with truth, and to 'turn off' the worldly messages that drove me to certain beliefs. Does that make sense? I decided to stick with nothing but praise and worship songs or just instrumentals. Eventually those songs stopped playing in my head and only the good songs remained. Now when the negative thoughts come, I just begin to sing praise songs, read the Word of God, or listen to a favorite praise song to avoid the dangers of losing heart.

Think about the songs you listen to today. I challenge you to look them up on the internet and read the lyrics word for word. Do they speak to you positively or negatively? You may be surprised at what the words are speaking to you. This was convicting to me as God showed me how I was mindlessly and willingly agreeing with the message not being conscious of it. I was shocked by this revelation and had to repent for giving myself to it willingly.

Decide for yourself if they edify or not, then get rid of anything that does not point you in a positive direction.

Next up, a powerful testimony, changed lives, and a great marriage. *DO NOT COMPROMISE YOUR INTEGRITY!* Stand strong and follow God no matter the cost.

But you [still] have a few people in Sardis who have not soiled their clothes [that is, contaminated their character and personal integrity with sin]; and they will walk with Me [dressed] in white, because they are worthy (righteous). (Revelation 3:4 AMP)

9

My Heart's Desire

I believe God was at work in me because I often found myself praying for Wayne. After divorcing, we spoke on the phone a few times regarding taxes or an insurance policy that needed some follow up and it was pleasant. There were no more sore words, and I began to feel compassion for him.

I had recently moved from a difficult roommate situation and was staying with my parents for a few days. What a mistake! One icy cold winter night, after an exhaustingly long day at work, I arrived at their home about 7:00 PM. I walked in with a grocery bag and my purse, chatted quickly about the day, and excused myself to the spare room where I was staying. I then took my grocery bag of four chicken breasts and put them in the freezer on the side porch. A few minutes later I went to talk to my parents and Mom was whispering a complaint to Dad about the food I had just put in the freezer. She told him I should have asked her first. I couldn't believe my ears. I thought this was so selfish and petty of my own mother and felt that sick feeling of rejection well up in me once again. I completely lost it. I was angry. I abruptly went back to the room, gathered up my belongings and headed for the door. My Dad blocked me from going out the front door and started yelling at me about how selfish I always was and how I didn't appreciate anything they had ever done for me.

I was shocked and dumbfounded at their actions, and just wanted to get out. The fact that I could never seem to please my parents was always a source of chagrin for me. Dad finally moved away from the door and Miss Roxy and I headed out to an unusual, and bitter, 20 degrees in good old Southern California.

I was crying hysterically, feeling yet again the sting of rejection and abandonment. Roxy girl and I drove around trying to figure out where to go when for some reason, I got the idea to call Wayne. I knew he was good for some friendly advice, and he was always a good listener. I stopped the car and talked with him for a bit, and he suggested Roxy and I find a hotel for the night. I felt an immediate sense of relief towards his recommended solution as my own red-headed rationale was near an emotional toilet-flush. He suggested I get checked in, have some dinner, take Roxy out for a pee, then get my pajamas on and call him back when I was settled. I did, and we had the most wonderful conversation that lulled me right into a warm and peaceful rest for the night.

Those were treasured moments I would not soon forget. I was grateful for his words of comfort and wisdom and took note of his caring involvement in helping to bring peace to a bleak and difficult situation. It helped calm me down. This was a trait in him that I appreciated, and one worthy of looking for when choosing a spouse. He told me he had found a church and was actively working on his own relationship with the Lord. We had sweet fellowship on the phone that night as we had so many times in the past, but this was different. We had compassion for each other.

Speaking for myself, I believe from that phone call on we began to see each other as fellow believers in Christ. I no longer expected him to be perfect and to 'fix me'. I was just beginning to understand that we BOTH were broken and bruised, and God's mercy was poured out to us because of it. I began to truly understand God's unconditional love and to reflect it toward others, especially Wayne.

We began talking on the phone often, mostly about God and how he was working in our lives. He was living in Long Beach at the time which was about two hours away. A few months later he was scheduled for a knee replacement and had to spend time in the hospital due to complications. He planned to come visit me nearly a month after his surgery even though he was not cleared to drive yet - he took buses and trains instead. It took him several hours. I was quite surprised by his sacrifice just after having surgery.

I will never forget how I felt when I saw him slowly walking up the street in his New York beret with head down, cane in hand carrying his backpack. When he lifted his head and looked at me, I thought I would melt into a puddle right then and there, Wow! He was truly the most handsome man I had ever met with the most gorgeous salt and pepper mustache and beard. Wayne had lost a lot of weight and was soft spoken. "Was this the same man I divorced?" I thought. I couldn't stop staring at him. I had a hard time believing this was the same man I was once married to. We walked to a nearby restaurant and had dinner. We went on and on talking about everything, better than the very first night we met. This time God was the center of our attention. Then and there I thought perhaps there may be hope for reconciliation.

Wayne had a life in Long Beach, and I had one in Fallbrook, but still he continued to travel the distance to come spend time with me. We would go for day trips with little Miss Roxy girl, because he missed her, and she missed him. He started coming to church with me almost every Sunday, and sometimes would spend the night, in the other room of course, because of the long distance.

A few months later, we started talking about remarriage and what that would look like. We agreed we were on the same page spiritually and wanted to grow in Christ and put Him first. We also still wanted the same things for our futures and missed being married to each other. We were grateful to have each other in our lives once again. Thank you, God!

Wanting to be in God's will, and in each other's arms, we quickly met with our pastor and his wife to talk about remarriage. They were our brand-new pastors who had just come from ministering on the island of Fiji in the South Pacific as missionaries. Their counsel was right on. They encouraged us to pray for each other, and to keep the Lord as our focus during our short three-month courtship. I remember one strong point our pastor made during counseling and that was to go into this with 'eyes wide open' knowing full well each other's strengths and weaknesses, and to count this ahead of time. We would have no excuse for quitting again. They were genuinely happy for us, and we quickly began planning our upcoming wedding. We were the first wedding they would perform in their new church home.

I never had a church wedding, and always wanted one. I felt that my previous marriages were cheapened because of this. We were originally married in a courthouse before the justice of the peace as I mentioned earlier. But this time I wanted my family and friends to witness our marriage ceremony in a church as it was sacred. So, we planned our wedding with family and friends and even wrote out our own marriage vows.

The pastor's wife also wrote us a beautiful song, titled: The Second Time Around. We both cried as we moved through the ceremony and spoke our declaration to commit our lives to each other once again. On June 7, 2014, our pastor pronounced us Mr. and Mrs. for the second time around. I felt like God was pleased with us and especially me.

Some dear friends of ours from the Pregnancy Resource Center where I worked planned and paid for a beautiful wedding reception. This couple volunteered thousands of hours for many years maintaining the Baby Boutique for our moms at the center. They were an important part of my life after Wayne and I divorced two years prior. Loved ones near and far came and we had a great time of celebration. It was beyond words. The welcoming love and support from family and friends left us overwhelmingly grateful for a second chance to love each other again, *The Second Time Around.*

The coming months proved to be challenging as Wayne travelled the 98 miles to and from work. He eventually gave up his apartment in Long Beach to keep costs down and stayed with friends or sometimes in his car. At first, he only came home on weekends because he started work at 6:00 a.m., and it was costly both financially and physically. He made huge sacrifices in the beginning just so we could be together. It was several months of this routine before I told him I wanted him home more often and we both agreed it was too hard. So, he started coming home every two days during the week and home on weekends.

Our church family prayed with us for almost two years after we remarried for a better work solution, and finally Wayne found a job closer to home, only an hour away. It was hard being away from each other, but God was faithful to hear our prayers and it was worth the wait. God's timing was sovereign as he used our difficult circumstances to mold and shape us both to trust Him above all else.

> *And we know [with great confidence] that God [who is deeply concerned about us] causes all things to work together [as a plan] for good for those who love God, to those who are called according to His plan and purpose (Romans 8:28*

AMP).

I wanted to save the best for last so that you could see how good God is when we wait on Him.

> *But without faith it is impossible to please him: for he that cometh to God must believe that he is, and that he is a rewarder of them that diligently seek him (Hebrews 11:6 KJV).*

No marriage is perfect, and neither is ours, but it is so worth it to be equally yoked, to be married to a spouse who loves God and realizes God's grace and mercy. Today our fellowship is sweet, and God has done amazing work in both of us. I still think sometimes that it is my husband's responsibility to fulfill the checklist of a great husband, but I quickly remember it's not. He is not God...and so, it is **easier to dethrone him and lift him up to God to whom he is accountabl**e.

The devil still lies and handcrafts accusations to divide us, but I find that when I pray and ask God to help my husband, he does.

> *My thoughts still go astray, much more often than I would like, but I am better equipped to **Declare My SOUL TO BELIEVE and My ENEMY TO LEAVE!** Now more than ever thanks to my mistakes.*

Remember, nothing is wasted, God uses everything for His

sovereign purposes.

Now we serve God together with a different attitude towards each other. It's called *GRACE*. God's Grace. We still argue; we still misunderstand each other at times; and we still stomp our feet and act like spoiled little brats. Well alright. Just me. But we give each other permission to be wrong and to be human with compassion.

The trauma of multiple marriages, or even one bad one, can be avoided by recognizing lies, behaviors, and triggers, and taking a different course.

There is always hope no matter what. Jesus paid the price on the cross. He knew what we would do in our lives and he died anyway, just for me and you. THAT IS real love!

10
Finding Your Husband

There has never been a greater need to address relationship problems than now. Here are some important statistics to consider while taking a closer look at the marriage commitment, and how a decline in moral values affects all of society today.

The High Failure Rate of Second and Third Marriages

Past statistics have shown that in the U.S. 50% percent of first marriages, 67% of second, and 73% of third marriages end in divorce. What are the reasons for this progressive increase in divorce rates? Theories abound. One common explanation is that a significant number of people enter a second or marriage 'on the rebound' of a first or second divorce. Often the people concerned are Vulnerable; they do not allow sufficient time to recover from their divorce or to get their priorities straight before taking their vows again. They enter their next marriage for the wrong reasons, not having internalized the lessons of their past experience. They are liable to repeat their mistakes, making them susceptible to similar conflicts and another broken marriage follows.[3] – Mark Banschick, M.D.

Remarriage in the United States

Between 1996 and 2008–2012, the share of those that had married twice or three or more times increased only for women aged 50 and older and men aged 60 and older.[4] – Jamie M. Lewis and Rose M. Kreider

Millions of Americans have been married three times or more.

As it turns out, serial marriage is a lot more common than you might think in the U.S.

According to Census data from 2013, over 9 million Americans have been married three times or more.

---

3 Mark Banschick, M.D. The Intelligent Divorce, February 6, 2012, © 2017, Psychology Today psychologytoday.com

4 Jamie M. Lewis and Rose M. Kreider, Remarriage in the United States, , March 10, 2015, census.gov/library/publications. Report Number: ACS-30

That works out to roughly 5.3 percent of the total married population. Or, put it this way: more than 1 in every 20 married Americans has taken three or more trips to the altar.[5] – Christopher Ingraham

Thrice-marriage rates by State:

Highest: Arkansas 10.8%

Lowest: New Jersey 1.9 %

September 3, 2015 – Christopher Ingraham

It's never too late to start new, no matter how bad it looks. If you woke up today, and there is breath in your lungs, you can be assured that God is on your side. Remember, your situation can change for the better in the twinkling of an eye.

> ***Hugely, the battle that wages on in our minds is due to a clouded vision created by our own focused thoughts. Change your thoughts based on God's truth instead of lies, and the outcome can only get better.***

---

[5] Christopher Ingraham, Millions of Americans have been married three times or more, September 3, 2015, © 2017 Washing Post News, Washingtonpost.com/news.

Let me encourage you with more truths from the Word of God: The devil accuses, but God has authority over everything.

> *Then I heard a strong loud voice in heaven, saying, Now it has come, the salvation and the power and the kingdom, the dominion, the reign of our God, and the power, the sovereignty, the authority of His Christ the Messiah; for the accuser of our brethren, he who keeps bringing before our God charges against them day and night, has been cast out! And they have overcome, conquered him by means of the blood of the Lamb and by the utterance of their testimony, for they did not love and cling to life even when faced with death, holding their lives cheap til they had to die for their witnessing. (Revelation 12:10-11 AMP)*

Let me be transparent for a moment. I don't count my life as cheap and I want to protect myself at all costs most of the time. My guess is you do too. This part is not up to us so please don't worry about measuring up on the proverbial measuring stick. He will do this work in you. Ask Him to work this in you. He will! My dear and precious friends in Christ, listen to Him, believe Him. He loves you with an everlasting Love. He will not disappoint.

I am convinced and confident of this very thing, that He who has begun a good work in you will [continue to] perfect and complete it until the day of Christ Jesus [the time of His return]. (Philippians 1:6 AMP)

If your life story is similar to mine in any way, and you are struggling to heal and have hope, you can now begin your journey to healing with the person of love himself. The embodiment of the word *Love* as we understand it is Jesus Christ. If you are just starting out on your journey to find the husband or wife of your dreams, I hope that this book has shed some light on some of the mistakes that can be avoided, and some of the lies meant to steer you in the wrong direction.

Let me repeat these final words to encourage you:

Lean on, trust in, and be confident in the Lord with all your heart and mind and do not rely on your own insight or understanding. In all your ways know, recognize, and acknowledge Him, and He will direct and make straight and plain your paths. (Proverbs 3:5 AMP)

Stay the course. Wait on Him, and when the going gets tough, and it will, throw yourself in His arms, and remember His Love and His provision just for you His Precious Bride. Read all of Psalm 104 to yourself or out loud if you must, to keep your mind stayed on Him.

Speak it and decide to **Declare Your SOUL TO BELIEVE and Your ENEMY TO LEAVE!**

Our Great God, Provider, Protector, Lover of our souls

Bless and affectionately praise the LORD, O my soul! O LORD my God, You are very great; You are clothed with splendor and majesty [You are the One] who covers Yourself with light as with a garment, Who stretches out the heavens like a tent curtain, Who lays the beams of His upper chambers in the waters [above the firmament], Who makes the clouds His chariot, Who walks on the wings of the wind, Who makes winds His messengers, Flames of fire His ministers. He established the earth on its foundations, So, that it will not be moved forever and ever. You covered it with the deep as with a garment; The waters were standing above the mountains. At Your rebuke they fled; At the sound of Your thunder they hurried away. The mountains rose, the valleys sank down To the place which You established for them. You set a boundary [for the waters] that they may not cross over, So, that they will not return to cover the earth. You send springs into the valleys; Their waters flow among the mountains. They give drink to every beast of the field. The wild donkeys quench their thirst there. Beside them the birds of the heavens have their nests; They lift up their voices and sing among the branches. He waters the mountains from His upper chambers; The earth is satisfied with the fruit of His works. He causes grass to grow for the cattle, And all that the earth produces for cultivation by man, So that he may bring food from the earth— And wine which makes the heart of man glad, So, that he may make his face glisten with oil, And bread to sustain and strengthen man's heart.

The trees of the LORD drink their fill, The cedars of Lebanon which He has planted, Where the birds make their nests; As for the stork, the fir trees are her house. The high mountains are for the wild goats; The rocks are a refuge for the shephanim.

He made the moon for the seasons; The sun knows the [exact] place of its setting. You [O LORD] make darkness and it becomes night, In which prowls about every wild beast of the forest. The young lions roar after their prey And seek their food from God.

When the sun arises, they withdraw And lie down in their dens. Man goes out to his work

And remains at his labor until evening. O LORD, how many and varied are Your works!

In wisdom, You have made them all; The earth is full of Your riches and Your creatures. There is the sea, great and broad, In which are swarms without number, Creatures both small and great. There the ships [of the sea] sail, And Leviathan [the sea monster], which You have formed to play there. They all wait for You To give them their food in its appointed season. You give it to them, they gather it up; You open Your hand, they are filled and satisfied with good [things]. You hide Your face, they are dismayed; You take away their breath, they die and return to their dust. You send out Your Spirit, they are created; You renew the face of the ground. May the glory of the LORD endure forever; May the LORD rejoice and be glad in His works— He looks at the earth, and it trembles; He touches the mountains, and they smoke I will sing to the LORD as long as I live; I will sing praise to my God while I have my being. May my meditation be sweet and pleasing to Him; As for me, I will rejoice and be glad in the LORD. Let sinners be consumed from the earth, and let the wicked be no more. Bless and affectionately praise the LORD, O my soul. Praise the LORD! (Hallelujah!) (Psalm 104 AMP)

My hope is that you have fallen deeply in love with Jesus and see Him as your husband, father, best friend, and provider. If so, keep Him close. Talk to Him moment by moment about everything, just as you do a good friend that you trust. He is better than any human being and can be relied on always to be there for you no matter what you need. Practice this daily and you will begin to feel His presence supernaturally in a way that can only be felt not explained, but you know is real.

Because he knows your heart, if you turn to Him in a moment of weakness or desperation, He will comfort you and give you peace and wisdom. When He does you will not forget it. You will turn to Him more and more. Every time you are afraid, you will be strengthened by Him. Stand on His Word and all will be well.

Maybe you are reading this book but don't know Jesus Christ in a personal way. Maybe you are looking for answers and don't have them yet. You can get all the answers you need. Just ask Him. It really is that simple.

And this is the confidence that we have in him, that, if we ask any thing according to his will, he heareth us: And if we know that he hears us, whatsoever we ask, we know that we have the petitions that we desired of him. (1 John 5:14-15 KJV)

If you want to know if Jesus is real, this is what the Bible says about him and how to give him your heart:

For God so loved the world, that he gave his only begotten Son, that whosoever believeth in him should not perish, but have everlasting life. (John 3:16 KJV)

> *For God so loved the world, that he gave his only begotten Son, that whosoever believeth in him should not perish, but have everlasting life. (John 3:16 KJV)*

(THIS IS HOW MUCH HE LOVES YOU)

For all have sinned, and come short of the glory of God. (Romans 3:23 KJV)

(WE ALL HAVE SIN AND CAN'T GET TO HEAVEN BY GOOD WORKS ALONE)

That if thou shalt confess with thy mouth the Lord Jesus, and shalt believe in thine heart that God hath raised him from the dead, thou shalt be saved. (Romans 10:9 KJV)

(ACKNOWLEDGE HIS DEATH AND RESURRECTION AND YOU WILL HAVE ETERNAL LIFE WITH HIM)

.

For whosoever shall call upon the name of the Lord shall be saved. (Romans 10:13 KJV)

(AGAIN, OUT LOUD IN JESUS NAME FOR ETERNAL LIFE)

Behold, I stand at the door, and knock: if any man hears my voice, and open the door, I will come in to him, and will sup with him, and he with me. (Revelation 3:20 KJV)

(HE IS COMING TO YOU AND WANTS YOU TO RECEIVE HIM INTIMATELY)

Jesus answered and said unto him, Verily, verily, I say unto thee, except a man be born again, he cannot see the kingdom of God. (John 3:3 KJV)

(ACKNOWLEDGE YOU NEED HIM AS LORD)

I tell you, Nay: but, except ye repent, ye shall all likewise perish. (Luke 13:3 KJV)

(BE SORRY FOR YOUR SINS AND ASK HIS FORGIVENESS)

If my people, which are called by my name, shall humble themselves, and pray, and seek my face, and turn from their wicked ways; then will I hear from heaven, and will forgive their sin, and will heal their land. (2 Chronicles 7:14 KJV)

(HE WILL FORGIVE AND HEAL)

Therefore, if any man be in Christ, he is a new creature: old things are passed away; behold, all things are become new. (2 Corinthians 5:17 KJV)

(YOU CAN BE A NEW PERSON FREE FROM GUILT AND SHAME)

If all this makes sense to you and you want to ask Jesus Christ into your heart to be your Lord and Savior, say this sinner's prayer and you will begin to know Him as He is:

> *Dear Lord Jesus, I ask you to forgive me of my sins and come into my heart to be my Lord and Savior. I believe you died on the cross for my sins and that you rose on the third day. Help me to live for you and make better decisions, amen.*

If you prayed this prayer, you are a new person in Christ. He will not let you down. This is the beginning of a new life where you no longer have to go it alone. Now, I recommend you get a bible you can relate to and read it. Ask God to help you find the right one for you. I prefer the King James version Open Study bible if you can find one. Look for a good church home where you can make good friends. Ask Him to help you. He will. He loves you more than any human being can or ever will.

Thank you for letting me speak words of life into yours, and may God richly bless you. May you find the True Love of your life, and True Peace that can only be found in Jesus Christ.

About the Author

Terri Lynne Corbett, born in Long Beach, California and the youngest of four daughters, struggled with identity and a deep desire for love and acceptance. After several attempts to find true love, and five failed marriages, she discovered how to break the cycles of bad relationships, marriage and divorce. She shares simple truths needed for healing and hope. Inside she's laid the stepping-stones to true peace, love, forgiveness, and finding true love in Jesus Christ.

She was a youth leader for ten years, and a mentor for at risk youth and adults for thirty-five years including a maximum-security facility for sexual predators and murderers. As Operations Assistant and Client Advocate for a pregnancy resource center for four years, she received training on how to encourage and help women who had experienced an unplanned pregnancy, and to realize their value through God's eyes. Terri also received extensive training on healing from the damaging effects of abortion through Surrendering the Secret. Currently she is a Volunteer National Leader for Life Impact Network founded by Pat Layton, author of the 8 week abortion recovery bible study Surrendering the Secret.

Her biggest joy is to encourage others. Her passions are personal and church group evangelism, healing for multiple marriages and dysfunctional relationships, abortion recovery, hospitality, cooking, eating, and fellowship with strangers and friends. She currently lives in Michigan with her husband of seventeen years, has two adult sons, and eight grandchildren.

Use Terri's tools to repair the damage from multiple marriages and bad relationships. Read the book to rebuild confidence and hope in who you are in Christ. Receive healing and a fresh beginning for you or someone you know today.

Declare Your <u>SOUL TO BELIEVE</u> and

Your <u>ENEMY TO LEAVE!</u>

The Daily 10 Grateful Essentials

Here we go again. Thank God. Another day Is ours!
Take 10 Grateful Essentials today with plenty of water (or Coffee), here they are. Drink Up and Be Healthy:

Grateful for the ability to breathe and move
Grateful for Purpose in Life
Grateful for Family and Friends who love me
Grateful for a roof over my head
Grateful for Clothing to keep me protected
Grateful for my five senses
Grateful for my emotions
Grateful for the ability to walk, talk, read & write
Grateful for food and daily provisions
Grateful for the ability to recognize all ten

Today is new! It's Not Yesterday. It's Not Tomorrow. Choose to Love You then Others. Eat Well. Work Hard. Play Often. Rest Plenty. Laugh and Cry when necessary it's the way He made you!

God Bless and Much Love from Terri Lynne!

To Order Supplies:

Magnets 4.5 x 5.5

Online at: www.wheresmyhusband.com

Made in the USA
Middletown, DE
02 March 2023